RAK-SU

Our Journey

MICHAEL JOSEPH
an imprint of PENGUIN BOOKS

OUR JOURNEY

with Martin Roach

CONTENTS

Dedicated to:

Our families, for always being loving
and forgiving, and for sticking with
and inspiring us every single day.

Welcome to our book!

Thanks for supporting us on our journey. Now it's our chance to share our story with you . . . Rak-Su is about four guys and one team, so in the pages ahead you'll hear from each of us, about our individual stories and how we got here, as well as how we came together as a band and stuck together. It's been an incredible journey so far, and it's only just beginning . . .

Q&A

jamaal

Q: Date of birth
A: 08/04/1992

Q: Height
A: 5ft 11

Q: Eye colour
A: Brown

Q: Star sign
A: Aries

Q: Favourite colour
A: Green

Q: One food you couldn't live without
A: Caribbean food

Q: Happiest memory
A: Watching cricket with my grand daddy

Q: Best thing about being in Rak-Su
A: The laughs and experiences we have

Q: Biggest dream for the future
A: To tour the world with my brothers and make new memories

Q: Favourite thing to do outside of Rak-Su
A: See friends and chill

Q: Strangest gift you've ever received
A: Soap

Q: Favourite album
A: *Confessions* by Usher

Q: First single you ever bought
A: 'Confessions' by Usher

Q: Favourite song
A: 'Something Special' by Usher

Q: First gig you ever went to
A: Chance the Rapper

Q: Best gig you've ever been to
A: The Weeknd

Q: Favourite Rak-Su Song to date
A: 'I'm Feeling You'

Q: Songwriter who has influenced you the most
A: Michael Jackson

Q: What social media do you spend the most time on
A: Instagram

Q: Who would you call in an emergency
A: Mother or Ashley

Q: Who in the band is the loudest
A: Ashley

Q: Who is the quietest
A: Mus

Q: Who is the messiest
A: Ashley

Q: Who eats the best/worst diet
A: Ashley/Mus

Q: If you could only watch one film ever again, what would it be
A: *Shawshank Redemption*

Q: One piece of advice you would give fifteen-year-old you
A: Find a hobby that you enjoy doing and do it for as long as you can

Q: Funniest onstage/backstage moment
A: Ashley falling down a hole in the stage during rehearsals

ashley

Q: Date of birth
A: 01/09/1991

Q: Height
A: 5ft 10

Q: Eye colour
A: Brown

Q: Star sign
A: Virgo

Q: Favourite colour
A: Anything bright

Q: One food you couldn't live without
A: I literally eat everything and just love all food

Q: Happiest memory
A: Performing at the Jingle Bell Ball having just won the *X Factor*

Q: Best thing about being in Rak-Su
A: Living a dream with three of my best mates from childhood

Q: Biggest dream for the future
A: A world tour and a Brit Award

Q: Favourite thing to do outside of Rak-Su
A: Play football

Q: Strangest gift you've ever received
A: A kosher cooking book for my birthday

Q: Favourite album
A: *2014 Forest Hills Drive* by J. Cole

Q: First single you ever bought
A: 'In Da Club' by 50 Cent

Q: Favourite song
A: 'Lights Please' by J. Cole

Q: First gig you ever went to
A: Dizzee Rascal

Q: Best gig you've ever been to
A: Stormzy in Paris

Q: Favourite Rak-Su song to date
A: 'Dimelo'

Q: Songwriter who has influenced you the most
A: Skepta

Q: Who in the band is the loudest/quietest
A: Me/Mustafa

Q: Who is the messiest
A: Me

Q: Who eats the best/worst diet
A: Worst Mustafa/best Myles, when he's not binging on buffalo wings or fried chicken

Q: If you could only watch one film ever again, what would it be
A: *Coach Carter*

Q: One piece of advice you would give fifteen-year-old you
A: It's OK . . . things are going to go wrong but you'll learn from them

Q: Funniest onstage/backstage moment
A: On tour Myles forgot his words, stopped rapping and said, 'Oh, wow!' It was hilarious

Q: Funniest *X Factor* moment
A: When rehearsing for Week 3 of the *X Factor*, I didn't look down and put my foot through a hole in the floor. Some people were concerned, most just laughed

Q: What would be your one luxury item if you were stranded on a desert island
A: Wi-Fi router

myles

Q: Date of birth
A: 11/09/1991

Q: Height
A: 6ft 2

Q: Eye colour
A: Green

Q: Star sign
A: Virgo

Q: Favourite colour
A: Purple

Q: One food you couldn't live without
A: Curried goat, rice and peas

Q: Happiest memory
A: Winning *X Factor*

Q: Best thing about being in Rak-Su
A: Doing what I love with my brothers

Q: Biggest dream for the future
A: World domination of the music industry

Q: Favourite thing to do outside of Rak-Su
A: Cook/gaming/play football

Q: Favourite album
A: *The Black Album* by Jay-Z

Q: First single you ever bought
A: 'Baby One More Time' by Britney Spears

Q: Favourite song
A: 'Annie's Song' by John Denver or 'All of the Lights' by Kanye West

Q: First gig you ever went to
A: Hear'Say

Q: Best gig you've ever been to
A: Jay-Z and Kanye West's Watch The Throne Tour

Q: Favourite Rak-Su Song to date
A: 'Wanna Tell You'

Q: Songwriter who has influenced you the most
A: Biggie, Tupac, Jay-Z, Dizzee Rascal, Skepta, Ghetts

Q: Who would you call in an emergency
A: Mum

Q: Who in the band is the loudest
A: Ashley (volume) or Jamaal (doesn't stop talking)

Q: Who is the quietest
A: Me or Mus

Q: Who is the messiest
A: Ashley

Q: Who eats the best/worst diet
A: Ashley/Mus

Q: If you could only watch one film ever again, what would it be
A: *Avengers*

Q: One piece of advice you would give fifteen-year-old you
A: Stay out of trouble and chase your dreams

Q: Funniest onstage/backstage moment
A: Me forgetting my lyrics and just saying 'Oh, wow!' in front of 13,000 people

Q: Funniest *X Factor* moment
A: Ashley falling through the stage

Q: What would be your one luxury item if you were stranded on a desert island
A: Phone

mustafa

Q: Date of birth
A: 02/02/92

Q: Height
A: 6ft

Q: Eye colour
A: Brown

Q: Star sign
A: Aquarius

Q: Favourite colour
A: Purple

Q: One food you couldn't live without
A: Crisps

Q: Happiest memory
A: Being in Egypt with my cousins – careless, free, fun times

Q: Best thing about being in Rak-Su
A: Living the dream/learning and progressing with my brothers

Q: Biggest dream for the future
A: Travel the world while performing

Q: Strangest gift you've ever received
A: Hair gel . . .

Q: Favourite album
A: *Donuts* by J Dilla

Q: First gig you ever went to
A: First and only gig I've ever been to was GoldLink at Electric Brixton

Q: Favourite song
A: 'My Own Plane' by Royce da 5'9"

Q: Favourite Rak-Su song to date
A: 'Pyro Ting'

Q: Songwriter who has influenced you the most
A: KRS-One, everyone in Wu-Tang Clan, Kweli, Tupac, Biggie, Royce da 5'9", Eminem, Talib, Lauryn Hill – so, so many to choose from!

Q: Who would you call in an emergency
A: My dad

Q: Who in the band is the loudest
A: Ashley for definite!

Q: Who is the quietest
A: I'd say me

Q: Who is the messiest
A: Ashley or me

Q: Who eats the best/worst diet
A: Best would probably be Ashley, worst I'd definitely say me

Q: If you could only watch one film ever again, what would it be
A: *The Longest Yard*

Q: One piece of advice you would give fifteen-year-old you
A: Keep going!!!

Q: Funniest onstage/backstage moment
A: Trying to find out what sound an armadillo makes

Q: Funniest *X Factor* moment
A: Ashley falling through the stage . . . after being warned there was a hole in it and to be careful

Q: What would be your one luxury item if you were stranded on a desert island
A: A fully working/fully fuelled helicopter . . . or yacht!

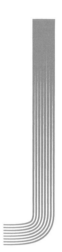

'Although none
of my immediate
family were
involved in music
professionally, or
even at an amateur
level, music was all
around me from
a very early age.
There were always
songs playing:
gospel, soul, R&B,
reggae, all sorts.'

I've always enjoyed being busy. When I was a little kid growing up in Barbados, we lived in a complex of flats next to a pasture. One day my parents bought me a toy lawnmower, and I used to go out into the field and mow the long grass, up and down, up and down, for hours, cutting absolutely nothing, of course, but I just enjoyed being busy and doing something fun.

Barbados is a nice place to grow up. There is a good mix of built-up areas but also plenty of forests and fields to explore. I was born on 8 April 1992, in a parish called St Michael, one of the biggest on the island. Unfortunately, not long after I arrived, my parents split up and then my mum and I went to live with my grandfather. I have three siblings, a brother and two sisters, all younger than me. We have always been a close family.

Although none of my immediate family were involved in music professionally, or even at an amateur level, music was all around me from a very early age. There were *always* songs playing: gospel, soul, R&B, reggae, all sorts. I grew up on artists such as Kirk Franklin, the Commodores, the Temptations, Bob Marley, music like that. There was also a lot of Soca, which is a style of music indigenous to the Caribbean. I guess my musical interests were quite varied for a young lad, but always very soulful and rhythmic.

'I used to go everywhere with music: if I was riding my bike, I'd be listening to music; if I was walking or running, I'd have my Walkman on; and I didn't even care if the CD skipped all the time!'

As I grew older, I developed my own taste in music as well as still listening to my parents' favourites. I discovered BET and that was pretty influential on me. Back then my usual day would be: get home from school, do all my chores, finish my homework and then the rest of the evening was mine until bedtime, so I'd invariably sit down glued to the television. As long as I had my Game Boy or TV and music, I was good!

When I was out and about, I had a silver Sony Walkman that I used to take everywhere with me. Back then kids my age didn't have mobile phones, so I'd have to upload all my parents' albums on to the single computer in the house (when it was my turn to use it for an hour!). Then I'd burn my playlists or whole albums on to a blank CD. I used to go everywhere with music: if I was riding my bike, I'd be listening to music; if I was walking or running, I'd have my Walkman on; and I didn't even care if the CD skipped all the time! That Walkman was pivotal to me having a constant soundtrack to my childhood. Music was something that kept me company, basically.

Church also played a big part in my young musical life. Everybody went up and sang in the choir, even if they weren't actually that good, we all just joined in. That was when people first noticed I could sing. Once my mum and her friends realized I had a good voice, they tried to get me more involved with the singing. There was no formal training, it was all very relaxed and encouraging. Previously church had been somewhere that I went and tried not to fall asleep, but once the singing started, that made it really fun, and I used to really look forward to that.

'That Walkman was pivotal to me having a constant soundtrack to my childhood. Music was something that kept me company, basically.'

Pretty soon I was singing all the time: in the bathroom, on the way to school, on my bike, in the fields, anywhere! I went to Grazettes Primary School in St Michael, but I didn't really sing or perform in the productions they put on; that would've been too public. I didn't really pay that much attention to my vocals in terms of a career or even as a major hobby. It was just for fun.

Cricket was a massive part of my life when I was younger, fuelled by my late and much missed grandfather, who was an umpire well into his seventies (all my grandparents really supported my sports and hobbies). In Barbados, cricket is a religion, it is something that is always around you. I grew up watching, playing and going to cricket. We'd play a game anywhere we could set up some makeshift stumps, whether it was with a school bag or a bin, whatever and wherever! We didn't have a proper red cricket ball so we'd use a tennis ball wrapped in electrical tape; we'd even try to shape the tape to create a seam around the centre. If no one had a bat, we'd pull a branch off a coconut tree, strip the leaves off and use the stem.

Weird Inside

I feel so weird inside
Baby you blow my mind
You got me on Cloud Nine
And I can't explain why
And I feel so weird inside
Baby you blow my mind
You got me on Cloud Nine
Woo Woo Woo Yeah Huh Uh Uh Uh Huh Uh Uh

I played for the school team and I was pretty good, but then I was hit in the face by the ball when someone bowled a full toss and I didn't see it coming until too late. The impact actually knocked me over the stumps and I was taken to hospital with mild concussion. I kinda went off cricket after that!

Away from sport and hobbies, I was a fairly avid Cub Scout (and then later a cadet). In class I studied hard and actually ended up getting grades among the top three or four kids in the final year. I then went on to Combermere Secondary School, and that was when I became really sports-obsessed. After suffering concussion in cricket, I got into basketball instead. I really enjoyed that and so did a lot of my friends, but the courts by my house weren't floodlit. It gets dark really quickly in Barbados and my parents couldn't always be sure I was safe, so I started to play tennis as well. We didn't have a school tennis team, but I used to train at the Ocean View Tennis Club. Unlike the local basketball courts, the club had floodlights, so we were able to train all year round. I would watch players such as Federer, Nalbandian, Nadal and Tsonga and try to emulate them on the local courts. I had a massive love for tennis during my early secondary school days.

'It never crossed my mind to be a musician – I loved music, don't get me wrong, but it was in sport that I imagined I would end up shaping a career.'

At this point, I desperately wanted to be a professional sportsman; I wasn't yet sure which sport exactly, but that is what I wanted to be when I grew up. It never crossed my mind to be a musician – I loved music, don't get me wrong, but it was in sport that I imagined I would end up shaping a career.

I really enjoyed my time at Combermere, it was a good school and I have very fond memories. Rihanna was actually a fellow pupil there, and she was also in the cadets. The school was well-known for cricket and some of my friends from there have gone on to play for the West Indies. Combermere also gained a reputation for developing sprinters: one of Barbados's greatest, Obadele Thompson, used to train there.

At this age I had my head in the clouds; at school I could get down to work when I needed to. Yes, I was more interested in sport than academic life, but I did reasonably okay with my studies. As the years went by, sport increasingly took over and my studies did slip a little, so instead of being in the top three, like at primary, I was in the top fifteen, then the top twenty-five. I wasn't a naughty kid, I just loved my sport. In terms of girls, I was a bit of a dork. I might like a pretty girl but I'd have absolutely no idea how to talk to her. So my life was literally just sport, music and studies.

Everything I did was soundtracked by music. By now technology had moved on and I was able to get a fake iPod, although it didn't work most of the time! No matter, I was always listening to music, headphones on, singing along. I wasn't performing (other than at church), I didn't write any songs, I had never been near a recording studio, I just listened to a *lot* of music. My musical tastes had really widened and I went through an alternative rock phase, listening to indie, pop-punk, Blink-182, All-American Rejects, Red Hot Chili Peppers. Outside of reggae, Soca and Latin music, many kids in the Caribbean are influenced by American pop culture. In fact

'Everything I did was soundtracked by music. By now technology had moved on and I was able to get a fake iPod, although it didn't work most of the time!'

the first album I ever got was *Confessions* by Usher; I must've listened to that record thousands of times! I used to play it cover to cover, day in, day out, and never got sick of it. Music was still very much under the radar, in the sense that I didn't perform in any public arena, but everyone knew that I could sing and that I was massively into my music.

I enjoyed music classes in school although I never really followed the theory; it just never stuck in my head. I flirted with playing instruments a few times. At one point I started playing the recorder, and I went everywhere with that thing. I played it all over the place, which I'm sure must've been really annoying! My dad then bought me a guitar when I was about thirteen and I tried to teach myself but that quickly fell away, it just didn't happen. I played the snare drum in the cadets, but instruments were never really my strong point; it was always singing that felt more natural.

People often ask me what Rihanna was like at school (back then everyone used to call her 'Fenty'). I wasn't big friends with her, but I knew her well enough to speak to. We all knew she was doing well – she used to sing in assemblies and school productions – but to be fair, I had no idea of the massive amount of work she was putting in behind the scenes. Then one day I was walking along behind the parliament building in town with my dad when she came running up and said, 'Shurland!' and told me all about what was happening with her singing career (people tended to call each other by their surnames, I don't know why). We were all really happy for her when she eventually got signed and went on to become the massive worldwide star that she is.

One time, after she had just put out her first album, she came back to perform in Barbados and, for some strange reason, I thought that after the gig she was going to come back to my house in a stretch limousine and whisk me off to be a famous star! Joking aside, her success made it seem possible that a kid from our school in Barbados could make it big, that dreams do come true.

In 2006, when I was fourteen, I moved to the UK with my mum and sister. My mum had moved over a year earlier to set everything up, get work as a nurse, find a house and sort all the practical things you need to look after a young family. Then twelve months later it was time for us to join her. My first impressions of England? It was the coldest place I had ever been! Oh my gosh, honestly! Apart from a trip to St Vincent in the Grenadines with the cadets, I'd never travelled before. I remember my mum giving me a thick scarf and heavy coat, saying, 'Jamaal, as soon as you get off the plane, put these on . . .' and I thought she was just fussing,

'My first impressions of England? It was the coldest place I had ever been! Oh my gosh, honestly! Apart from a trip to St Vincent in the Grenadines with the cadets, I'd never travelled before.'

'Initially I was quite sad about moving to England. I missed my friends, obviously, but it was more that it felt so cold, wet and dreary. It was just not what I was used to in Barbados.'

like mums do, but wow! I think I stepped out of the plane at Gatwick, felt the cold and stepped right back in! We trudged off the plane and had to drive for what felt like hours. I just remember seeing all these red-brick houses, they all looked the same, the rain was teeming down and it was so cold and damp.

Initially I was quite sad about moving to England. I missed my friends, obviously, but it was more that it felt so cold, wet and dreary. It was just not what I was used to in Barbados. It wasn't a culture change that I could ease myself into: we left Barbados and all my family and friends in the heat, and eight hours or so later – bang, we landed and it was freezing and wet, and we were in a place where the only people I knew were the people inside my house.

My mum had set up home in Watford, just north of London. Obviously I didn't know anyone . . . but I still had my music. It was when I moved to England that I got my first phone with a few songs on it. I also remember my sister had a portable speaker that looked like a massive pill; I think it had 256MB of storage on there, which at the time was enormous! 'You can get almost thirty songs on there!'

'Because I was new and didn't know the timetable, I had no sports kit with me. They sent me to the lost-property cupboard and I had to kit myself out with all these odds and ends; there weren't any trainers so I ended up wearing my black school shoes. So there I was, shivering on this slippery bit of AstroTurf, wearing a mismatched bunch of lost school clothes, when this kid walks up to me and says, "Hello, I'm Mus."'

Mum enrolled me in the local secondary school, Westfield, starting in Year 10. Since I was the new kid, I got put in the bottom set for everything, because the teachers didn't know where I was at intellectually (over time I worked my way up to the top sets). Despite my reservations about the cold and the rain, I actually settled into life in England fairly quickly. I made a lot of friends in my first week or two – in fact, on my very first day at my new school in England I met a guy called Mustafa Rahimtulla. We had PE, but because I was new and didn't know the timetable, I had no sports kit with me. They sent me to the lost-property cupboard and I had to kit myself out with all these odds and ends; there weren't any trainers so I ended up wearing my black school shoes. So there I was, shivering on this slippery bit of AstroTurf, wearing a mismatched bunch of lost school clothes, when this kid walks up to me and says, 'Hello, I'm Mus.'

We got talking and, if I remember rightly, we later sat by each other at lunch. After that we were instant friends, we just clicked. I soon found out that Mus could beatbox and dance, which I thought was really cool, although at this very early stage there was no talk between us of doing any music, we were just mates hanging out. He lived in Cassiobury Park, which meant my house was on his way home, so we used to walk back from school, usually stopping off at Ambala, the best chip shop in Watford!

Through Mus, I started to meet lots of other people and so my circle of friends grew pretty quickly. I didn't really tell anyone that I enjoyed singing, though, even Mus. Although we already listened to some of the same music (he was into hip-hop, which was a big influence back home), he really educated me on music you could pop and break to, and our musical tastes became more intertwined over time.

Mus used to do breaking in Watford and one time he invited me down to a class – he always wanted everyone to dance, basically. I'd never really got into dancing and it wasn't something that I imagined I would ever be particularly good at, but it was something to do so I went along. I learnt how to six-step and go into a baby freeze, but apart from those two moves, that was the beginning and end of my dancing career!

Some days I'd go from Mus's house to see one of his friends called Myles Stephenson. I knew Myles from school, mainly from being on the basketball team together, and we hit it off immediately. Quite soon I was spending a lot of time at Myles's house because he lived just a fifteen-minute bike ride away from mine. I knew that Myles wrote lyrics and rapped, but I didn't know anything more than that and we were never in a position to make music together. We'd usually meet other friends locally and play basketball in Croxley.

'I knew Myles from school, mainly from being on the basketball team together, and we hit it off immediately.'

A pivotal moment in my quietly evolving music career came when the school did their own *X Factor* talent show. I didn't actually watch TV talent shows at the time – I was still very much into my sport – but the school competition was a fun idea. Me, my best friend Michael and another guy called Ali formed a group called Jamaali – the name came from mixing up parts of all our first names, but I think I got the best deal! This was my first proper public performance so it really sticks in my mind. We performed Justin Timberlake's 'Señorita' (just like Rak-Su later did on the real *X Factor*!); if I could have been anyone famous at that time, it would have been Justin Timberlake (or maybe Usher). We rehearsed and tried to approach the show professionally: we dressed up in similar clothes and knew the track off by heart. I am a big Pharrell Williams fan as well as being into Justin, so I'd heard the song a million times already.

The most amazing moment came when we got to the chorus and the audience started singing the words back to us! When the song ended, the hall erupted – we went down a storm! Everyone went crazy, and people were coming up to us afterwards saying how cool it was and how great we sounded, it was almost as if we were celebrities. That was such a buzz. The performance was filmed but, sadly, not long afterwards someone broke into the school and stole all the footage. Even so, that was a big moment for me; I really enjoyed the performance, and obviously being so well-received was a great boost. I can't remember if I felt nervous beforehand or not, but I vividly recall how good it felt performing onstage, that was just the best feeling. We even won £100 of vouchers to spend at the Harlequin Shopping Centre in Watford, so it really did feel glamorous, ha ha!

Occasionally we also used to sing in school assemblies in a mixed choir. One time I was asked to be the lead vocalist for a version of 'I Believe I Can Fly'. So that was another public outing for my singing and I really enjoyed that, too, but I still had no active plans to move into music as a career. I just loved singing for the sake of it.

After secondary school, I stayed on at the sixth form. I started posting a few cover songs on YouTube with Ali, who could sing a little bit as well. Interestingly, we started getting some attention – even friends of mine back in Barbados were watching these clips and commenting positively about them online. So I posted a few more and they got even more attention, and it became apparent that people were enjoying my singing.

I was still obsessed with sport, though. My love of basketball had been reignited in England because it was much easier and safer to play than on the dark courts in Barbados. A lot of my friends were big into the game, too, so by the time I was around seventeen I had ambitions to become a professional basketball player. I trained and played for hours and hours every week; I went to some fairly serious training camps and the standard was very high. Basketball really shaped my life to be honest, because the people I played with tended to be a lot older than me and they ended up becoming some of my best friends. They had more mature views on certain topics and ideas, and that inevitably influenced how I approached life.

One day I went round to the house of a friend, a guy I played basketball with, and he had a small music studio set up in his bedroom. He knew I loved music and enjoyed singing, so we recorded an original song called 'Find Your Love'. I couldn't tell you what the verses were about, I just remember the chorus, something along the lines of 'Find your love for me, find your love for me, baby, so that we can be together!' I chuckle about those lyrics now, but to be fair, little did I know, that was the start of a deeper involvement in music that would eventually change my life forever . . .

'FIND YOUR LOV'

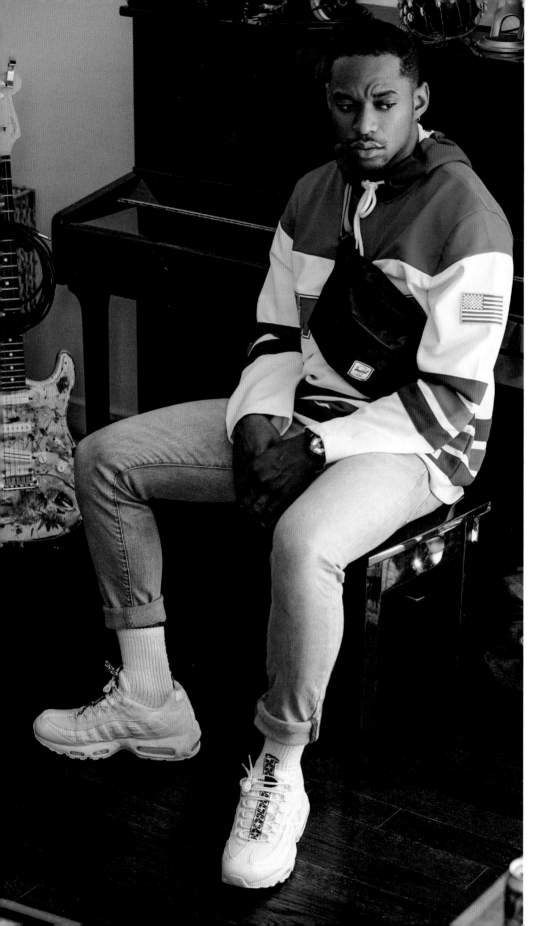

Back at one of the numerous basketball training camps I attended, my coach said that if I could get some travel money together I could go to Gran Canaria and play for six months, and if that went well I might even be drafted into a pro team. On the one hand, this was a really exciting prospect; however, I knew I couldn't go because in the meantime I'd applied to loads of universities to study physiotherapy – my love of sport had led me to a point where the idea of a career in physiotherapy was really quite appealing. I wanted a career in physio or basketball, not music, that was how I looked at it. I loved music but it didn't seem possible that I could make a career out of it, so I'd applied to all these unis but every single one turned me down! To be fair, I think it was my grade U in biology that put them off. Definitely not ideal!

Eventually Brighton Uni messaged me and said I could take Sport and Exercise Science, which wasn't quite the same as physiotherapy but I was pleased to have an option. I had a good time in the first-year halls of residence. My housemates knew I could sing because I was always playing music and singing along to it, but I certainly didn't join any bands or make myself known as a performer. My time at uni was okay but when I'd finished I went back to Watford and got a job as a health care assistant at the hospital where my mum worked. I also got a job at Argos, so I was balancing two jobs at the same time; it was pretty exhausting. Some days I'd work a twelve-hour shift, go home, sleep for three or four hours, wake up and then do another shift. Sometimes it worked well, but other times I was just walking around like a zombie.

Somewhere in the midst of all this I met a local guy who I'd competed against in athletics many times. I'd seen him around Watford a lot growing up but away from athletics we only really crossed paths at a few parties. He seemed like a cool guy and Myles knew him well. He was called Ashley Fongho.

'Somewhere in the midst of all this I met a local guy who I'd competed against in athletics many times. I'd seen him around Watford a lot growing up, but away from athletics we only really crossed paths at a few parties. He seemed like a cool guy and Myles knew him well. He was called Ashley Fongho.'

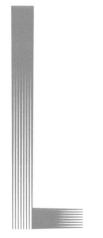

ASHLEY

'I was born on
1 September 1991.
My little brother is
six years younger
than me, so at
first it was just
me and Mum.
We bounced
around a few
places in my early
childhood, starting
off in London.'

M y mum has always been such a hard worker. She came over to the UK from Cameroon and was intent on getting herself qualified. While she was studying to get her nursing degree, she had to take on jobs at the same time to bring money in; not long after she graduated, I was born, on 1 September 1991. My little brother is six years younger than me, so at first it was just me and Mum. We bounced around a few places in my early childhood, starting off in London. As she had moved over to the UK away from family, Mum didn't really have much of a support network, so understandably at times the workload was too much to handle on her own and I did spend some time with foster families when I was younger. Overall it was a happy experience – I just saw them as my family, and I guess because of that I had a slightly unorthodox idea of what a family was.

By the time my little brother came along, we had moved together as a family to Islington, then my little sister arrived a few years after that. We moved once more, to north Watford, and that is where my family eventually settled permanently. Early on we didn't see too much of Mum. We didn't know it at the time but the reason why sewed a seed for us. We learnt hard work was good and saw sacrifice daily. My brother, sister and I love her, and are really thankful for it now.

I actually always liked school, to be honest! Even though we moved around a fair bit, I think I was a lucky kid growing up. Playground rules dictate that if you are good at sport then your life is a little bit easier, and fortunately I was quite good at football. Also, you tend to do okay if you don't mind having a fight sometimes to protect yourself!

At Parkgate Junior School I studied reasonably well and did okay in class. I never liked having to do homework, but I guess that's not unusual! I really loved creative writing and poetry, I loved playing with words. One time there was a competition of some description, I can't remember the full details, but I do recall that my poem was submitted for a national award, which made me feel really proud. That also got me thinking that it was cool and fun to play with words and not be frightened of using them to be creative. As a kid I never stopped talking, so for me writing was just an extension of that. In fact, I often found it easier to write things down than say them to someone in person.

In Year 6 I was part of a rap 'group'. We had a teacher who had come over from Australia and he organized for me and three other boys to do a little rap. The song was really short and my verse was: 'I've got a flavour and my name's Ashley Fongho, gonna shoot like Man U, so you better get ready. It's warm in Cameroon, so why am I here? I've got the Parkgate flavour, ain't gonna disappear.' Technically that is the first song I ever wrote and I can't believe I can still remember every word!

'As a kid I never stopped talking, so for me writing was just an extension of that. In fact, I often found it easier to write things down than say them to someone in person.'

'I'd lie on my bed and listen to that album over and over, for hours and hours, just hearing the words 50 Cent was using, the way he wrote and the stories he was telling. Perhaps inevitably that fuelled my formative attempts at rapping, nothing serious. I genuinely didn't think about wanting to be a rapper, I was just a kid messing about. I guess that was an evolution of the poetry I'd been writing since I was at primary school.'

Around this time a family friend called Solomon took me out shopping and he said, 'I'm going to get you a CD – you can have any one you want.' I ended up getting the most recent *Now That's What I Call Music*. However, he also bought 50 Cent's *Get Rich Or Die Tryin'*, a slightly different vibe! Naturally I was never going to be allowed to buy that, but once we got home I took it from him anyway and loved it! I'd lie on my bed and listen to that album over and over, for hours and hours, just hearing the words 50 Cent was using, the way he wrote and the stories he was telling. Perhaps inevitably that fuelled my formative attempts at rapping, nothing serious. I genuinely didn't think about wanting to be a rapper, I was just a kid messing about. I guess that was an evolution of the poetry I'd been writing since I was at primary school.

Music was always there throughout my childhood. My Aunty Nicky (who has sadly passed away) played R&B, constantly! She got me into the habit of watching MTV Base and The Box, and I would sit for hours and hours watching those channels. It wasn't because I wanted to be in music as a career at that point, I just loved watching the videos and listening to the songs. I suppose urban music such as R&B and, to a degree, hip-hop, just became embedded in me.

My fascination with music carried on into Bushey Meads Secondary School, where I did okay in class. By then I was more outgoing, I would say. In fact, as I headed into my teenage years I was a bit of a strange personality! I enjoyed school, I had a laugh and a joke, although I have to be honest here and say I got loads and loads of detentions. I was put in isolation more than a few times and even got suspended for fighting; to explain myself, when I was younger I felt like I was invincible and I had a little superhero complex. If a bully was picking on a smaller kid, I kind of took it upon myself to step in and stop that. So with most of the trouble I got in, a lot of my teachers knew why I had been in a fight and were never really that angry at me. To be fair, most of the punishments were actually for not doing homework or for being a bit too lively in class. Even when they dished out detentions, they were usually smiling because I wasn't straight disruptive, just a little over-zealous. Also, although I was in detention fairly regularly, I was also in the top set for most subjects. I did enjoy school and I would like to think that if you spoke to my teachers most of them would have good memories of me.

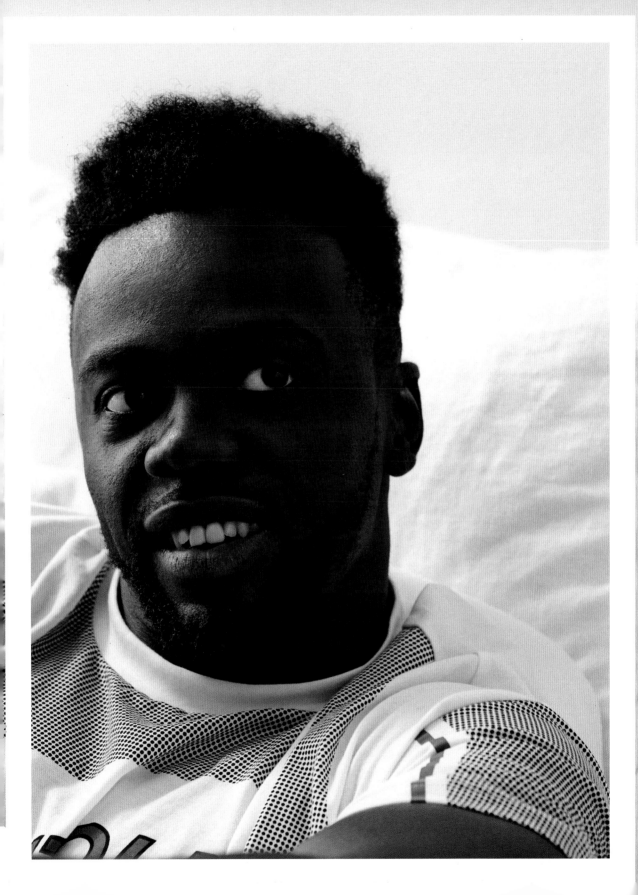

If you'd bumped into me in the secondary school playground, you would have found someone who was quite loud and just didn't shut up! I haven't changed that much, I really haven't! I had a lot of friends scattered around in different groups and cliques, rather than one big gang of my closest mates. (It's funny, because being in Rak-Su is the first time I have ever had a single friend-ship group.) Oh, and you would often have seen me with a duffel bag full of milkshakes, cookies and chocolate bars from Costco, which I would sell around the playground and actually make decent money from!

Probably the single biggest part of my secondary school life was sport. I was obsessed! Football was always my main passion but I was also pretty good at athletics (especially the triple jump). I was really good at basketball, probably because I just grew a lot faster than everyone else (I've been the height I am now since I was fifteen). I even tried cricket, but in all fairness I was absolutely crap at it.

Around this time my mum had set up a nursing recruitment business, which stabilized us as a family. She started it from her bedroom and I have watched her build that company up from the ground, and I am incredibly proud of her for doing that. I think my mum is a superhero for going through everything she did, raising me and my siblings pretty much alone, all whilst starting her own business! From quite a young age, I thought it would be a pretty cool idea to take what she had done and then expand and grow it into a massive conglomerate. I didn't actually know how I was going to do that, but it was always in my mind to try.

Throughout my teens, sport and music remained the twin loves of my life. In Watford the local authorities ran a website called 'Mouth to Mouth', which was an open forum that loads of the schools in the area used. The idea was that it was a secure and monitored place to set up a page and chat to your friends, to socialize and stay safe online. Quite a few kids used it to have rap battles, so we'd literally type in all our best lyrics and have these online battles in full digital view of all our friends. We also started doing battles in the playground as well, so it was getting really exciting at this point. Again, I hadn't thought of rapping as a career, I was just a teenage kid who loved his sport and music, and especially enjoyed doing both with friends.

'I was just a
teenage kid
who loved
his sport and
music, and
especially
enjoyed doing
both with
friends.'

One of the kids I was friends with but who went to a different school was called Myles Stephenson. I didn't know to what degree he was writing lyrics at this point, but we got on well because we played football against each other and sometimes basketball; we were competing against one another from about the age of seven. Myles was at Westfield School, along with Mustafa and Jamaal, so I also got to know them over time, too. We were all part of a big mixture of mutual friends, into football, music, hanging around Watford; it was a cool group of mates. Myles used to live around the corner from me in north Watford, so we would go down the park on a Friday night or just hang around in the town centre. Me and Myles often had day trips to London, even when we had no money to buy anything. We would get the train in and have a wander around the shops, just watching people and hanging out. There was a little Chinese place in Oxford Street where we would always end up with a takeaway . . . great memories.

It was perhaps inevitable that some of these mates would start to record some of their lyrics. Again, it was nothing too formal, but one friend had a studio set up in his bedroom just around the corner from my house, so we'd go round there and record some stuff. Sometimes Myles would be there, sometimes he wouldn't; same with me. It was all very casual. The first song I recorded with Myles was called 'Blazin' MCs' – it was all right, ,so we put that out on MySpace and all my friends bantered me about it terribly! To be fair, it was okay, and the feedback we got online wasn't too bad, but I did get some stick all the same.

Me and Myles spent loads and loads of time with each other growing up and had a lot of experiences together, through sport and also just as mates hanging out. For example, one time we both went down to Dagenham for a football trial, which was a really memorable day. Unfortunately we both got told 'no' by the football scout, so on the way home we ate our body weight in KFC – if I remember correctly, we bought a big bucket each! It wasn't always sport, music and messing about, though. One

'Me and Myles spent loads and loads of time with each other growing up and had a lot of experiences together, through sport and also just as mates hanging out.'

'Mus would often try and teach me dance moves and I would sometimes go to dance classes, but in the end I kind of gave up because I could never get a handstand right, so I thought, *This is useless!*'

time we went to a house party where there was a big group of pretty confrontational people who didn't like the fact we weren't white and – without going into detail – we ended up legging it out of there for our own safety. That was pretty scary, to be honest, but I guess, looking back, it forged even more of a bond between me and Myles, so from then on we were completely intertwined. I'm glad to report that it isn't like that any more in those parts of Watford, which can only be a good thing.

I have always enjoyed meeting people and making new friends, and one of those lads around town was Mustafa. Initially he was just another person who was always around, and he knew Myles because they went to the same school. I knew Mus was involved in a dance crew and I thought that was cool, so we just ended up being really good friends from that. That led to us going to teenage parties and spending time with each other and the friendship just grew. We recently found a phone video of one time we ventured down to the High Street: Mustafa is beatboxing while I'm rapping. It was just a laugh – we never had a conversation about working together in a band, we were just messing around.

By sixth form, Myles and I were playing a ton of football together, especially after he started going to my school, Queens', so we became very close. There was another friend called Max who used to dance with Mus, so we were all really good friends. Mus would often try and teach me dance moves and I would sometimes go to dance classes, but in the end I kind of gave up because I could never get a handstand right, so I thought, *This is useless!*

Jamaal doesn't fully come into my story until later, which is funny because of how close we have ended up becoming. We sort of loosely knew of each other when we were younger but I didn't spend much time with him during our middle teens. He probably knew of me because I had a big mouth and was always messing around, being loud. However, I didn't really get to know Jam until we were quite a bit older. That's probably because Jam was a good kid, he wasn't hanging around in the street doing nothing or in parks messing about. Jam's still a good guy; he's an angel.

'From a creative point of view, I loved the culture of writing sixteen bars, spitting what you've written with a group of friends and seeing who was the best, clashing with each other.'

I was big into hip-hop for quite a long time, but one day around 2004 I heard Wiley's 'Wot Do U Call It?' and that had a *massive* impact on me. I just thought, *What is this song? Who is this guy? This is amazing!* After that I just devoured every grime video and song I could find. I was on YouTube all the time, looking up every corner of the scene. I was completely bowled over by the whole grime vibe: the music, the lyrics, the atmosphere, everything about it. In a very short space of time, grime was something I became very, very passionate about.

From a creative point of view, I loved the culture of writing sixteen bars, spitting what you've written with a group of friends and seeing who was the best, clashing with each other. I found that really fun. As a sports fanatic, I always liked the competitive side, so that edge just appealed to my nature and made grime even more essential.

I think my instinct to write my own material comes from growing up listening to, initially, hip-hop and then grime. In both genres, the most important elements of the songs are *what* you are saying and *how* you are saying it. So to have someone else write your material just doesn't fit, it isn't authentic; that approach has always been looked down on in those two worlds. You don't cover other people's stuff, you write your own, that's just what you do.

I was pretty obsessed with grime, to be honest. At this point I had an admittedly narrow taste in music, always grime, R&B and hip-hop. That was what I knew, that's what I listened to, that's what my head was rooted in. By contrast, Myles was the complete opposite; he would – and still does – listen to all sorts!

A load of us would always watch the online channels and see what was happening on the scene down in London. Then a couple of people started their own YouTube channels, with people rapping over grime instrumentals (some of it was hip-hop as well). Over time some of them would be sending for each other, trying to start clashes with other people, mostly just saying whatever they wanted to say, and it got pretty competitive. Then the various online sites started competing for views and feedback – we all wanted to know who was the best spitter in Watford; there was such a buzz. Up until that point Watford hadn't really had a music scene, so it was very exciting to suddenly find there was a great vibe around town.

Some of the lyricists could get pretty brutal in their criticism of people, and others said things that occasionally caused issues, but I never said anything bad in any of the music I was involved with. I've always kind of had the mantra: *How would I feel if my mum heard this?* Some people might say that isn't very rock and roll, but that's just how I felt.

I got quite heavily involved in all of this; me and my friend started up a channel and we'd go around filming people, then editing the videos and posting them. I like seeing people around me do well, I love to see friends achieve and progress. I was always happy to be involved and if I saw people trying to do something and I thought I could help, then I would.

'I've always kind of had the mantra: *How would I feel if my mum heard this?* Some people might say that isn't very rock and roll, but that's just how I felt.'

————————————

However, this fantastic momentum and enjoyment sort of stalled when I left sixth form and went to study psychology at Loughborough University. I went because it is one of the top sports universities in the world, so that was a big draw. I'd just started playing semi-pro football and that was still a very big part of my life; Loughborough offered the chance to continue that sporting progression at a high level. With regards to a longer-term career, I was wondering about corporate finance or possibly heading back to work with Mum in her business.

Unfortunately, the three years I spent at uni were not good times for me. For starters, being away from home pulled me out of all the exciting stuff happening on the Watford music scene, though I did end up making some music with a few people at Loughborough. Their style was far more emotional than anything I'd done before, which was cool because it opened me up to a different lyrical approach. Nothing significant came of that, but it was good to be learning, all the same.

Actually, if I am being completely frank, I would say my time at uni was the worst three years of my life. I spent the whole of my first year with a front tooth missing after an accident playing football. So, yeah, not cool being at Freshers' Week with a front tooth missing and a brace fitted! There were also some difficult private challenges going on in my family, and seeing people I love go through that was difficult. I had a girlfriend who I was completely head-over-heels in love with, but when things went sour between us that kind of hit me quite hard. In Watford I'd been a big fish in a small pond in terms of sport, and suddenly I wasn't even making the uni football team first XI, which really frustrated me. There was a level of football I wanted to get to and it wasn't happening; I think I played for the first team once. It was just crap, I felt like an idiot.

'When I got back to Watford a switch just flicked in my head and that was it, I was like, *I'm going to change this, I'm sorting this out, I will not stay feeling like this!*'

So I wasn't in a good place for most of uni, and this was an unusual feeling for me. Previously, I'd always been the one to find the positives in any situation, that is my nature, but at uni I struggled to do that. With every earlier knock-back in life, I would find the positives, get my head down, work hard and get sorted. However, at uni, for the first time I went the other way and kind of disengaged. I went from being a kid who was always busy to suddenly having way too much spare time on my hands to think about what was going on. When I was around other people I was still the same 'me', energetic and loud, so no one really cottoned on, but when I was by myself I got super-duper introverted. I stopped going to lectures, stopped playing semi-pro football for a while as well, and just became really lethargic. At times I felt like I was underwater. Nothing was fun. Somehow, I still wrote music, although my material became more reflective and emotional, maybe even darker. Academically, I had always been good during school, I had always been fine, but when it came to my finals I got a 2:2 and, for me, that just wasn't good enough. I didn't even go to my graduation because I didn't feel proud of what I had done for three years. Rightly or wrongly, I felt like I'd failed myself at university. (I would eventually go to the autumn ceremony after my mum and uncle forced me to!)

Coming out of uni, I basically said to myself that I had to change, I had to get back to my best and I was determined not to fail at anything again. I don't really know how, but when I got back to Watford a switch just flicked in my head and that was it, I was like, *I'm going to change this, I'm sorting this out, I will not stay feeling like this!*

Flights

Chilling on a day to day we wont definitely boss

but shh we're trying anyway,

Stop me man that aint the truth, stop me now I'm talking
loose

I just love the vibes at studio when I'm inside the booth

I just love the feeling when we're up ~~on the stage~~
upon a stage

Way before the getting paid, we were surfing on our wave

Catch us at a festival and things wont be the same

To my girl I'm guarenteeing you that I will never
change!

X Ash

What I did was go to work for one of the biggest recruitment businesses in the country, hoping to eventually get a job within my mum's business. I am proud of how I bounced back because I was totally on it, almost immediately. I got my head geared up straight away and quickly did really well at work. I started to get my mojo back at football too, I was back to being myself in terms of feeling happy and fun, I really worked hard and made the most of every single day.

There were three things I wanted to get right in my life: one of them was to be successful at work; secondly, football-wise I always felt that I should play at the level of the Southern Premier League or higher; and thirdly, something very significant dawned on me when Jamaal came into my life properly – I had spent the last God knows how many years making music but I had never done anything serious with it. I wanted to create and write a body of musical work that I was really proud of.

I said to myself, *These three areas of my life are going to go well, no ifs, no buts, no maybes. I don't care what it requires, how many hours it is going to take, this is going to happen.* So I knuckled down at work and my mum and family were really proud of me. I felt like I had redeemed myself. Football – I did the same thing. I started three leagues below where I wanted to be, but over the course of two years I ended up playing for a team called Chesham in the Southern Premier League, which was the level I had always wanted to achieve.

So that just left one more area of my life to get right, a passion I wanted to throw everything into so that I could say I was proud of what I had achieved: my music . . .

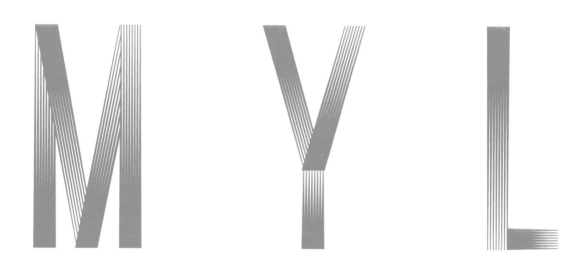

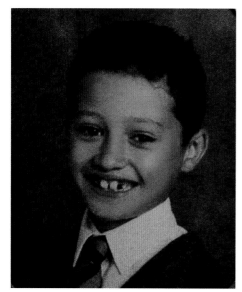

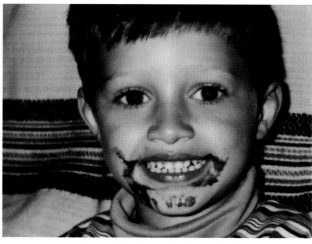

'I was listening to reggae artists such as Gregory Isaacs and Duane Stephenson, records like Duane Stephenson's *Cottage in Negril*, stuff like that. There weren't any musicians in my family, but both my parents were always playing records.'

M

y parents had normal jobs: my English mum was anurse and my dad was a doorman who had travelled over from Jamaica to set up a new life in England. They met at the gym – Vale Farm. My mum was a gymnast and my dad played for the reserves at Wasps Rugby Club. I was born in Watford. In later life when sport, and in particular football, was something I actively pursued as a career, I guess you could look back on their skills and think it must have had an impact on me, in terms of being around parents who were so active and physically capable.

I was born on 11 September 1991, but sadly, around seven years later, my parents got divorced. After that I stayed with my mum in Watford the majority of the time, and went to see my dad in Greenford, west London, every Wednesday and once on a weekend. Some years later my mum remarried and my new stepdad had two children from his previous relationship, so I inherited two new siblings; later they had a baby together, too. Dad also remarried, and that brought along two more stepbrothers, so I became part of a pretty big extended family!

Unfortunately my dad had to stop playing rugby following a car accident, which must have been a great shame for him at the time. He worked the doors at local clubs, which is a tough job. Although obviously I was nowhere near old enough to be around the nightlife my dad worked in, the music he heard at those venues he would also play at home, so that was a big influence on what I listened to. From a young age, I was listening to reggae artists such as Gregory Isaacs, records like Duane Stephenson's 'Cottage In Negril', stuff like that. Both my parents were always playing records. One of Mum's favourites

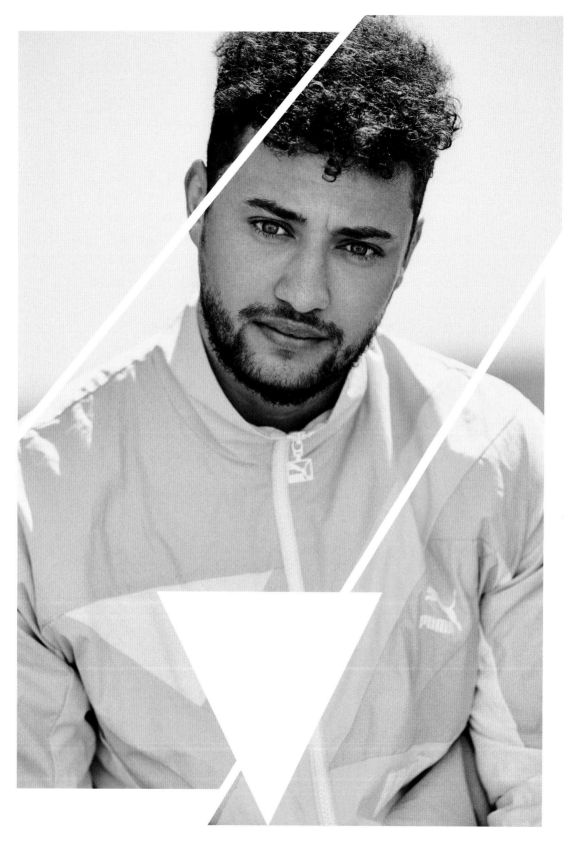

that also became one of mine is a fairly unusual choice for a kid who grew up in Watford – I absolutely love John Denver. He was an incredible singer-songwriter, best known for his folk and country-style music. He actually wrote over 300 songs and has sold millions of records over decades. His lyrics are really fascinating – they are all about relationships and storytelling, you can just listen to his songs and instantly picture the characters and situations. His country voice is also dope, and the instrumentation is really simple, almost basic, but absolutely perfect. There was never any huge, over-the-top production on his songs, it's just very stripped back and simplistic. Some of his lyrics are so specific, too; for example, he talks about how he used to go to his grandma's house and stay on a massive goose-feather bed. Really raw and authentic. Every year we would go camping or snowboarding and it would literally be John Denver's album on the way there, then playing all week while we were away and then back on again in the car on the journey home. In terms of more modern music, Mum got me into artists such as Dido – also a storyteller – but to be honest, I love *any* style of music. I've never really been a fan of just a few narrow genres – for example, believe it or not, just before I was working on this chapter, I was chilling out listening to some Mongolian throat singing and then some pirate songs! I love hearing different musical styles from all over the world; I think you can learn something from all of them.

'I love hearing different musical styles from all over the world; I think you can learn something from all of them.'

As a really young kid, as much as I loved all these different types of music, I never once thought I'd be involved in music a career. I didn't really think about the future in that way. Primary school wasn't a particularly easy time for me. Originally I went to Watford Fields, but when my mum and stepdad got together I had to move to a new school, Ashfield, in another little village called Bushey, where I stayed until Year 6. Moving schools at that young age is never easy, but I was a troublesome kid anyway. I was a handful, to be fair. Maybe it was because my parents had split up, I don't know. I could be cheeky and naughty, although I think I knew there were certain boundaries I couldn't cross – certainly with my parents; I knew not to overstep the mark there. At school though, I was a little more challenging.

The teachers knew I could be trouble, but I still had a good relationship with them as I wasn't exactly badly behaved. I also had a lot of friends at school and part of the reason for that is because from an early age I was good at football. I supported Newcastle United initially, because my uncle was a fan and they played the first match I ever went to watch. When I started playing myself, it turned out I was pretty good. So when I moved school, this was a great help, because if you can score goals and play well, it makes it easier to interact with people and make friends. Football really helped in terms of me settling into each new school. It was much more than a hobby though – for as long as I can remember I wanted to be a professional footballer. That was the dream.

'As a really young kid, as much as I loved all these different types of music, I never once thought I'd be involved in music as a career.'

I wasn't top of the class at primary school, then when I moved up to secondary school, Westfield, I did okay, my grades were what I would call average, not bad but not amazing. It was all about my football. I played every spare second I could, training several times a week, playing more than one match a week, also kicking a ball about at every break and dinner time, after school at the park, just football, football, football. I played a fair bit of basketball, too, but football was my main obsession.

By this age my musical taste was broadening out even more. My stepbrothers were into more indie-style music, artists such as Kate Nash, so I definitely listened to that, but then I also got quite heavily into pop-punk like Sum 41 and Busted. My first ever gig was actually Hear'Say, the pop band who were formed from the original *Pop Stars* TV talent show, which came before *The X Factor*. I went with my two stepbrothers, my mum and stepdad. At the same time I discovered hip-hop, so I would listen to albums by the likes of Tupac, The Notorious B.I.G., pretty varied tastes! I sometimes wonder why I like such different music, and I think part of it is that back then we all had to share one computer, so whatever music anyone had down-loaded, you tended to chuck on a USB stick and listen to that.

'In terms of meeting the other lads in the band, I'd been playing football with and against Ashley since the age of about seven.'

In terms of meeting the other lads in the band, I'd been playing football with and against Ashley since the age of about seven. We were both football mad, so in a town like Watford, where there was a very good, strong football scene, it was inevitable that we would cross paths. We had the same friendship group of Watford boys, too. I kind of became best mates with Ash from the age of about ten, along with a third kid called Kyle. We used to roam around Watford, getting up to no good! Nothing serious, just messing about.

With regards to my teenage football, I think it's fair to say that I was the best player in the school. I was playing for the sixth-form team (with boys sixteen to eighteen years of age) when I was in Year 9 (aged about fourteen). I got trials with Crystal Palace because of school team performances, but I wasn't able to attend; they didn't let me go because my grades weren't good enough.

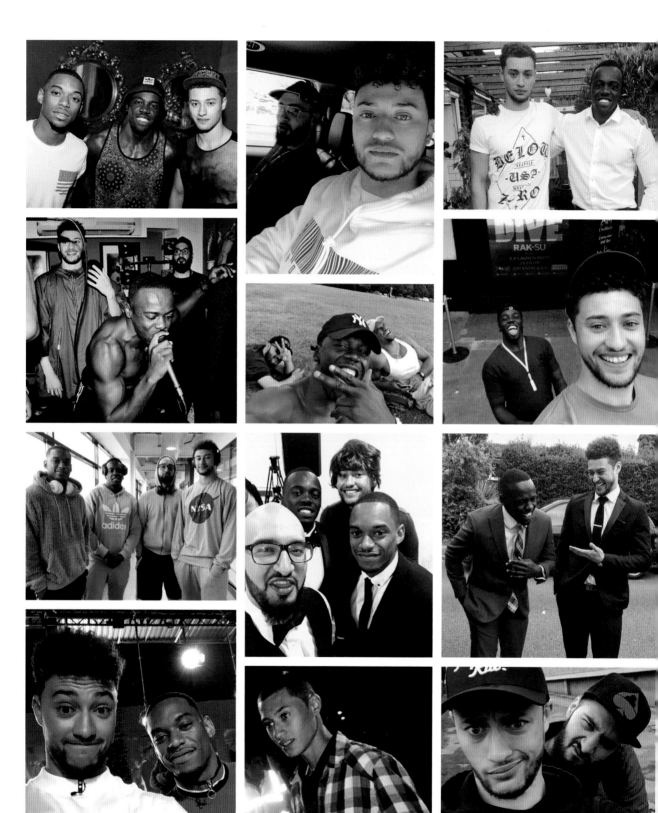

It was early on in secondary school that I met Mustafa and then Jamaal. I was good mates with Mus from about Year 7, hanging out at school and around town. Then one day in Year 10 this kid called Jamaal turned up from Barbados – that caused a lot of excitement at school, I can tell you! Everyone was talking – 'Oh, yeah, have you seen that new boy from Barbados?!' – and all the girls fancied him. I thought he had a funny part-American accent and a terrible haircut, but that didn't seem to stop everyone liking him! He was really good at basketball, so we met through that and soon became close mates.

'I could relate to some of the stories they were telling; they were by people who lived in the same sort of places that I did, walked the same sort of streets. It felt like grime was detailing the story of a life that I was kind of living.'

———————————

Around 2004, a new style of music came into my life that had a massive impact: grime. Growing up in Watford and west London, it was hard not to notice grime. I guess in a way there's the same element of storytelling as in the John Denver songs that I love, even though the two styles of music couldn't be more different. I loved the way an MC would tell a story so fast – seventeen syllables a bar! – but at the same time still so in-depth, while also keeping a rhythm and following a melody; it felt more melodic and rhythmic than some of the hip-hop and rap I was listening to.

I heard these grime songs and loved the music and artists straight away. At this early stage, as well as the big artists, such as Wiley, it was the underground names, people on the street that I came across. I could relate to some of the stories they were telling; they were by people who lived in the same sort of places that I did, walked the same sort of streets. It felt like grime was detailing the story of a life that I was kind of living. They'd describe the council estates that I would be hanging around when I went to my dad's in west London – it was just so refreshing to hear stories I could relate to. When I was listening to B.I.G. or Tupac, for example – who are incredible – I couldn't relate to their tales of New York or the West Coast. By contrast, it was exciting to hear someone rapping about Ladbroke Grove or White City; that really hit home. I really bought into the whole vibe. I found grime just so exciting.

There'd be grime clashes that you could go to watch, but you had to be very careful where you went because that genre could be very territorial. There were a lot of amazing grime artists in east London, but if you were a west London boy, then it wasn't necessarily a good idea to go across town. You had to really think about where you were going, because if you did turn up at a clash and people didn't recognize or like the look of you, it could spell trouble. I watched a lot of grime clashes on YouTube and was just blown away by how good these people were.

What is sick about grime is that everyone writes their own stuff. Most people's lyrics were rubbish at first, but kids were just finding their way and, to be fair, the spitting is fast.

In terms of trying to write my own lyrics, I was no different from any of these kids. That said, how I actually came to start writing my own lyrics is quite unusual. As I said before, I had moments at school when I was troublesome. In fact, I'm going to be really honest with you here and tell you that at one point I started attending anger-management classes. I wasn't a bad kid, don't get me wrong, I just got frustrated quickly sometimes. Anyway, there was this guy running these anger-management classes who rented out a studio in Watford, and he asked me and a few other kids on the course to write lyrics over a garage instrumental. We all walked into the studio to see this massive mixing desk, all this amazing equipment, vocal booths, microphones – to kids who were struggling through their mid-teens it was really impressive. I vividly remember looking at the studio engineer and thinking, *Waoh! He must be really famous!*

'We all walked into the studio to see this massive mixing desk, all this amazing equipment, vocal booths, microphones — to kids who were struggling through their mid-teens it was really impressive.'

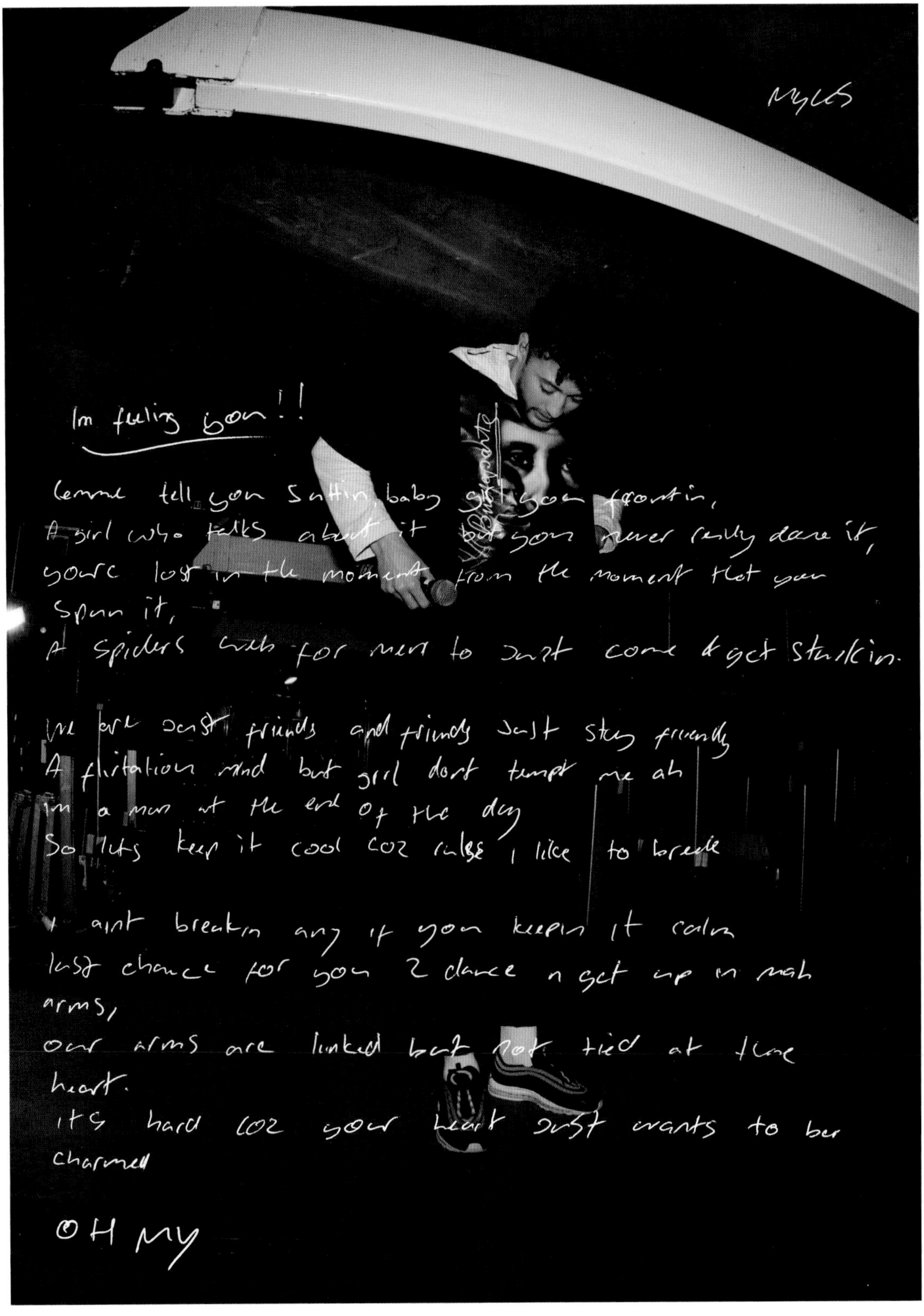

Myles

Im feeling you!!

Lemme tell you suttin, baby girl your frontin,
A girl who talks about it but you never really done it,
youre lost in the moment from the moment that you
spun it,
A spiders web for men to just come & get stuckin.

We are just friends and friends just stay friendly
A flirtation mind but girl dont tempt me ah
im a man at the end of the day
So lets keep it cool coz rules I like to break

I aint breakin any if you keepin it calm
last chance for you 2 dance n get up in mah
arms,
our arms are linked but not tied at the
heart.
its hard coz your heart just wants to be
charmed

OH MY

The idea was to write positive and encouraging words, to make us think about our situation in a helpful light. The music was really fast and the space for the words made them pretty quick, too, so it was quite a challenge, but we went in there and had a great time having a go. I wrote all this stuff about staying on at school and reading all your books, studying hard; I tried hard to do what they were asking of me. I actually really enjoyed the experience – it was fun getting into a studio, and all these years later I can see that giving us the opportunity to do that was very cool. That was the first time I ever wrote and recorded my own words. How pivotal that is now, looking back . . .

From that moment, I wanted to write as much as possible. My stepbrother spat lyrics and recorded, too: one time we went to Poundland and bought a USB microphone, took that home and started rapping to instrumentals. The funny thing was, in our room there was only one chair, so we'd sit half each on the edge, writing and rapping while trying not to fall off! We were actually embarrassed about recording our lyrics, so we would only do it when my dad had gone out.

I started to learn some production software because I found it all so interesting, and that obviously helped, but I didn't tell any of my friends what I was up to. I really enjoyed building up the skippy flow, trying to practise a lot of syllables in one bar and elements like that. I found it really challenging and exciting. I wasn't writing to be famous or make money – I didn't even tell anyone that I constructed these lyrics – I just enjoyed putting my thoughts down on paper.

'It was fun getting into a studio, and all these years later I can see that giving us the opportunity to do that was very cool. That was the first time I ever wrote and recorded my own words. How pivotal that is now, looking back . . .'

'My future bandmate Ashley loved grime, too. That was all he ever used to listen to! Perhaps inevitably, at some point one of us showed the other a few words they had written and we very loosely said, "Okay, why don't we try some recordings?"'

———————

The amazing and beautiful part of grime is that there is no hiding behind stuff, not behind instrumentation, not behind lyrics; it's a very open and honest style. It is also very personal – the artists say what is relevant to them – so if you were to rap someone else's words, you weren't rated and would probably get slated for it. Cover versions are usually looked down upon, you'll be sussed out straight away. For me, the beautiful thing about grime is that if you want to be a credible artist you have to write.

My future bandmate Ashley loved grime, too. That was all he ever used to listen to! Perhaps inevitably, at some point one of us showed the other a few words they had written and we very loosely said, 'Okay, why don't we try some recordings?' It wasn't about being in a band together or making a career out of it, this was just for fun and to be doing stuff with your mates. So we ended up going to the house of one of our mates, who had a studio. Well, I say 'studio' – he had literally taken all his clothes out of a wardrobe, then soundproofed it with all this sound-deadening foam and taped a mic up the side and over into the top. We'd take turns squashing into this rickety old wardrobe to record some lyrics. The first song we recorded (as Ash has said) was called 'Blazin' MCs', which was just the worst song we have ever made, and I think I am right in saying no one else but me still has a copy – not even Ashley!

A while after that we formed a movement called TBM, which stood for 'The Brotherhood Movement'. This was twelve of our closest friends who had grown up together around Watford who could all MC or rap. We were on social media, we wore our bandanas and always chilled together, it was sick. During our early teens the grime scene had been very London-based and everybody wanted to be like the artists you saw and heard about in the city. However, we started to want to represent our home town and, to be fair, Ashley was the main guy who said, 'Right, let's make something of this for Watford.' So the main focus was to get our freestyles out there, make songs with each other and try to build up the music scene in Watford.

'The amazing and beautiful part of grime is that there is no hiding behind stuff, not behind instrumentation, not behind lyrics; it's a very open and honest style.'

'Running parallel to this, my football career was progressing really well throughout my teens. I played football probably at least five, often six days a week.'

Running parallel to this, my football career was progressing really well throughout my teens. I played football probably at least five, often six days a week. When I moved up to sixth form, I kept pushing with the football and also, I'm proud to say, I stepped up with my studies as well. I preferred it to high school, because although I didn't clash with anyone it was a rough school, where you would have to defend yourself at times. However, in sixth form I enjoyed my football, had a good circle of friends, studied pretty hard and did okay with my grades. I eventually graduated up to the semi-pro Middlesex County Football League, a shift up in quality and an achievement I was very proud of and passionate about.

My football continued to progress, so that I was selected for England Schoolboys, which was obviously something that made me very proud. As you can imagine, at that point my dream was still to be a professional footballer, and when I started playing for Hayes & Yeading in the Conference South league, that seemed to be a viable option. I was dedicating my life to football and I thought I had the drive, but actually, looking back on it now, I realize that I didn't have anywhere near as much drive for football as I do for music. However, I was doing really well and progressing up the ranks, so it was an exciting time.

I used to listen to music on the way to games and then in the changing rooms to hype myself up, usually something like Jay-Z – he was my favourite artist for a long time. Songs like 'Public Service Announcement' were on constant rotation. I was still writing and scouring the internet for great instrumentals. I then started immersing myself more and more in the production side, teaching myself all about the software and really getting into the technical detail. I think production suits my personality – I can be quite obsessive about small details, so I enjoyed finding little pockets of where to put instrumentation and capturing a sound perfectly.

It was a really hectic, exciting and at times exhausting period of my life, but I loved every minute: tons of football, great friends and, all the time, soundtracking everything, there was music – that was always my constant companion.

MUSTAFA

'I never learnt an instrument – my biggest connection with music during my childhood came not through singing or playing an instrument but through dance.'

Music was everywhere during my childhood. My parents weren't musicians – Dad is an accountant, Mum used to be a PE teacher – but they loved music so it was always around me. I believe my nan could play the piano; she apparently had a very good musical ear. My parents are from Egypt, so there was a lot of Arabic music on in our house, but the family home was in Colindale, London, so they would also listen to current and older English artists, all sorts. I was born on 2 February 1992, and when I was about eight my family moved to Watford. From a very young age, I would go every year to Egypt for the summer holidays, so I soaked up a lot of cultural influences there, too, not just music. Even so, I never learnt an instrument – my biggest connection with music during my childhood came not through singing or playing an instrument but through dance.

Soon after we moved to Watford, my older brother watched a 1984 street dancing film called *Breakin'* and began dancing. I started noticing this around the time I was in Year 3 or 4, and essentially just copied him. At that time a lot of people were breakdancing, it was still kind of the 'in' thing. I was fascinated, so I began to try some of the moves myself. I just loved it straight away.

At first I just learned the basics but over time I began to understand the connection between dance and music in more depth, how different sounds would suit different movements. My style started off as breakdancing, and then I got into popping as well. I never went to any dance classes, I just watched my brother and his mates; that was a great way to learn. My brother took me to a place where they would hire out a local hall, play some music and everyone would swap ideas and teach each other. It was great. It was never a dance class with one person choreographing a piece, it was literally just whatever you wanted to learn or work on that night. They all kind of helped each other out, which was very cool to be around. At this point I was mostly dancing to hip-hop breakbeats, it wasn't until I started popping that I was dancing to funk, so artists such as Bootsy Collins, the Gap Band, George Clinton, Funkadelic, Zapp & Roger, as well as hip-hop and R&B.

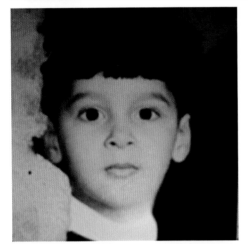

'I was born on 2 February 1992, and when I was about eight my family moved to Watford. From a very young age, I would go every year to Egypt for the summer holidays, so I soaked up a lot of cultural influences there, too, not just music.'

I used to play a lot of football and tennis but dancing quickly took over. My first ever public performance was at a primary school disco; I remember dancing to So Solid Crew's '21 Seconds' in Year 4. I only did about three or four moves on repeat for the whole song but everyone went crazy! Looking back, it was probably awful, but everyone seemed to enjoy it, and the next day the head teacher came into the class and gave me a sticker that said 'Head Teacher's Award'.

In 2006 my brother took me to my very first dance competition, the UK B-Boy Championships in Brixton, London. I hadn't even known that these events were going on. I'd previously watched a lot of these guys on YouTube and copied the way they dressed as well as danced, so I was very excited to actually be going to an event. We queued outside Brixton Academy for about three hours just so that we could get a good spot to watch. I remember walking in, looking around the venue, listening to the sounds, soaking up the vibe; it was so busy and cool, plus everyone was super-friendly. Once the competition started, there were dancers from all around the world — it was incredible! The dance community is relatively small, so there is a real sense of friendship even when people are competing against one another, and I just totally bought into that whole vibe. It's a shared passion, something that everyone in the venue loves. I was in my element, it was such a great day. That was dancing on another level, all these people competing against one another, dancing in ways that I had never seen before. I was absolutely mesmerized and I remember thinking, *This is what I want to do.*

'I wanted to do cool stuff that would surprise people and make them think, *Wow, how did he do that? I didn't even know people could move like that!*'

'My brother wasn't into beatboxing at all, but it was something that had completely captured my imagination, separate to the dancing.'

People have different ways of dancing, especially in competitions. At first, I just wanted to look cool. I wanted to do cool stuff that would surprise people and make them think, *Wow, how did he do that? I didn't even know people could move like that!* A lot of dancers judge their style on the groove and the feeling that you have when you dance; over time I realized that I needed to get the right balance of doing cool moves but also having the groove and the foundations of the movement. Popping and breaking in particular have foundations and if you aren't doing those right, anything else that you do isn't going to work. It's going to be just too superficial. Those competitions were such amazing places to learn. Don't get me wrong, I still want to look cool and make people wonder!

What was also really interesting about that first competition in Brixton was the beatboxing, as it was my first experience of it. I saw this guy on the mic doing some crazy stuff which was apparently all coming from his mouth! I was completely bewildered and blown away. I had absolutely no clue what was going on. Turns out he was a brilliant and well-known beatboxer called Beardyman. That night I got straight on the internet and looked him up, then discovered performances by artists such as Faith SFX, Rahzel (considered the godfather of beatboxing by many), Killa Kela, and a whole bunch of other people. My brother wasn't into beatboxing at all, but it was something that had completely captured my imagination, separate to the dancing.

It is pretty unusual to dance and beatbox – I don't think I knew anyone who did both – but I just loved that dual passion. At first my efforts to beatbox were hilariously bad! It is a big leap from listening to someone beatboxing to trying to make those sounds yourself. There wasn't anyone around to give me lessons so I had to figure it all out myself. Initially I just thought of a really simple beat and kept repeating that over and over again until I could nail it, then I'd add a little something extra and just kept building it up and up like that. Your voice is a muscle, the more you work it, the better it becomes and the more you can control it, so like everything in life; it's all about practice and hard work. Mind you, I think my parents found it really annoying that I was constantly walking around the house making all these strange sounds twenty-four hours a day! I used to beatbox while I was watching the TV, doing my homework, in the shower, going to the bathroom . . . I think it really tested their patience!

'By this point I was fascinated by anything to do with this corner of youth culture, the so-called 'five pillars' of hip-hop: rapping, DJ'ing, graffiti, beatboxing and breakdancing.'

One day I was practising and a friend of mine was nodding his head and I remember thinking, *Ah, okay, so it isn't annoying him, he's actually enjoying it!* That's when I knew I was on to something and so I just doubled my efforts to practise even more.

Back in Watford, my circle of friends who were into dancing was getting pretty good. Initially I wouldn't say it was much of a crew, but as we started getting progressively better we said, 'Let's actually do something with this.' By this point I was fascinated by anything to do with this corner of youth culture, the so-called 'five pillars' of hip-hop: rapping, DJing, graffiti, beatboxing and breakdancing. I was only thirteen, but I'd found something that I wanted to be a part of and I just wanted to discover as much information about it as possible; I wanted to learn *everything*. I wanted to get into DJing, I wanted to rap, I wanted to learn how to do the different styles of graffiti. But it was the dancing and beatboxing that I seemed to want most (with DJing soon to come!).

At school, by contrast, I was fairly reserved, although I had a good circle of friends. I could dance and play football reasonably well, so I was fairly popular, which was obviously a nice feeling. I also used to get private lessons with a maths teacher and that really helped, too. At this point I was heading towards a career in accountancy, which seemed like a natural path for me, given my dad's job and expertise. My parents have always been very supportive and naturally they wanted me to be financially secure and in a good profession. So it's perhaps understandable that they didn't necessarily appreciate my passion for dancing, and they were certainly right in thinking it isn't an easy way to make a good living. The financial rewards just aren't the same as some sports and other areas of the arts, and your career tends to be over quite soon – many elite dancers retire between the ages of thirty and forty.

I know many amazing dancers who still have a second job, which is kind of weird when you think about it. If you were to pick the top ten singers in the country and compare their earnings with those of the top ten actors and the top ten dancers, you'd be very shocked at the difference. So you really have to dance because you *love* to dance.

The challenge for me growing through my teens was that as much as I completely understood my parents' desire for me to be an accountant, I wasn't driven to follow that career path. It didn't seem right for me, and it just didn't appeal to me in the same way as dancing.

In Year 8 I went to a private American school in Egypt for a large part of the academic year, which was quite challenging. In England I was known as the Egyptian one, and during that stay in Egypt I was known as the English one, so I felt a little bit like I was a tourist in both countries (I'm fluent in spoken Egyptian). During my Egyptian studies, the school held a talent competition, which was won by a very polished sixth form band who'd done quite a few gigs. I managed to come second, which made me really happy. I still have the trophy in our house in Egypt!

My dancing really started to develop during my time at Westfield Secondary School. Everyone knew that I could dance and beatbox, word kind of goes around pretty fast. It was also at secondary school that I met two other lads who would change the course of my life. In Year 7 I met a guy called Myles Stephenson who was really good at football, and we quickly became firm friends. Then one day (in Year 10) I walked on to the AstroTurf for a PE class and there was this new kid standing there in his school shoes and a mish-mash of PE kit and I thought, *Who's that?* That was the first time I met Jamaal. He hadn't long moved to the UK from Barbados and so I went over and said hello. The three of us got on really well and would quite often hang around together outside of school hours, too.

'That was the first time I met Jamaal. He hadn't long moved to the UK from Barbados and so I went over and said hello. The three of us got on really well and would quite often hang around together outside of school hours, too.'

I knew Myles was into his rapping; I'd never seen him performing anywhere but he was into that whole vibe. I also found out that Jamaal could sing, *really* sing. I first realized how good he was when we all did a talent show at school. His trio won the singing trophy and I won the dancing, which I did solo, with a little beatboxing thrown in.

By the time I was taking my GCSEs I was dancing all the time; it was pretty much an obsession. I had started entering competitions myself and that was a real eye-opener, but it also fired up my passion for dancing even more, because I enjoyed the rivalry and competitive environment. A typical competition will see around fifty people enter, they all dance once and then the judges choose a top thirty-two or sixteen to go through to the 'battle' stages. Initially you only get to dance for about 30 to 45 seconds, so you don't have much chance to show off what you can do. If you get chosen for the battle stage, you will usually dance against one other person in a straight knockout. At my very first competition I ended up in the quarter-finals against my best friend, and he won! I was really pleased for him and a little bit gutted myself, obviously. I kind of knew it was either me or him who was going to win the competition, but I consoled myself with the knowledge that he was a couple of years older than me so I had time to learn. I always went away from competitions on a positive note; even if I lost, I'd just train harder, work more, research deeper.

Gradually I started winning a few of the battles, then a few more stages and soon I was in semis and eventually finals. Then, in 2008, at the UK Hip Hop Crew Championships, I won my first major competition: that was a *big* moment. I managed to win the Varsity category, the under-18s freestyle. I also entered the popping category, which was open to all ages, and I even got into the semi-finals of that. That was the day that I figured, *I can actually do this.* The success just made me want to do it even more.

Some of the more high-profile dance competitions I ended up doing were overseas, in countries such as Portugal, Germany and France, so that was a really cool way to travel. As an interesting aside, where you come from kind of determines the way that you dance. So the dancers from France will be different to the dancers from America, Portugal, Japan, the UK and so on. Going to these competitions and spending time with different people was brilliant – I am someone who learns well from watching, so going to these overseas events was great for introducing me to a much wider and more unusual variety of styles and ideas. The French dancing style had a big influence on me. For example, probably the biggest single influence on my dancing was a man called Salah – if it wasn't for him, I don't think I would be popping at all. He won *France's Got Talent* – the first dancer to win anything mainstream and commercial. He did that just by making people laugh, making people happy, and that's what I wanted to do; I wanted to make people enjoy what they were watching, as well as think, *Wow, that's amazing!*

I always tried to highlight the less obvious parts of a song with my dancing, to hit little bits that people perhaps don't realize are there until they watch you dance. To do that, I had to research and find a song that I liked, which was increasingly dictated by the producer rather than the artist. It can get quite niche when you are trawling through thousands of songs looking for unique beats by little-known producers, but I just love all of that. That's how I ended up appreciating the work of producers such as the late great J Dilla, among many others. I have always wanted to research dancing and beatboxing as much as possible – to me, if you love and are interested in something, then learn the history, find out how it started, see who's doing what and how; it's fascinating, and at the same time your love for the subject will only grow even more.

Meanwhile, my friend Myles was getting better and better at football, and one of the lads he used to play against was this really chatty guy called Ashley Fongho, so we got to know one another through our shared group of friends. Also, whenever we all used to go to someone's birthday party, me and Ashley were usually the only two not drinking, so we made a connection with each other; we'd sit and chat and grew close that way.

'Whenever we all used to go to someone's birthday party, me and Ashley were usually the only two not drinking, so we made a connection with each other; we'd sit and chat and grew close that way.'

When we were in Year 11, someone recorded a phone video of me and Ash at the top of Watford High Street, me beatboxing and him rapping. During those secondary school days, it wasn't a case of any of us saying, 'Hey, let's make music together' – it just kind of happened. It was fun, we were all learning and trying stuff out. It was really loose and relaxed. Likewise, Jamaal and I would often do videos of me beatboxing and him singing covers; we just enjoyed posting the videos online for fun.

Back in the world of dancing, there were a lot of competitions in London that I entered and, as I consistently improved, I won a few of them. At the same time, some mates and I formed a crew called Toy Boxx, which was the first time that we created a choreographed sequence as a crew. Before that, most of what we had been doing was freestyle. We seemed to gel and so started entering – and winning – competitions. Over time, we progressed to a pretty high level, eventually coming second in the World Hip Hop Crew championships in Vegas (sadly I didn't go, but that's another story – gutted!).

The competitions kept coming thick and fast and my crew kept winning. One win at Camber Sands earned us £1,000 prize money, which was the first time we'd made cash from doing what we loved. Mind you, by the time the money was split about ten ways, and all the travel and accommodation costs deducted, there wasn't much left for each of us!

We were becoming pretty well-known in dance circles and several of us were also doing solo competitions at the same time. Part of the appeal was that we were Watford boys – most of the top crews were from London, so being from outside of the city gave us an edge. When we beat those London dancers, the city boys would all be like, 'Who on earth are these guys and where did they come from? They just came out of nowhere!'

After a while I had to leave Toy Boxx because I just wasn't making it to training enough with my school work, plus when they competed in London I couldn't always safely make the journey or find the spare cash for train fares. After a few months though, some friends – Luke Lentes, Lee Putman, Luke Bailey and Isaac Kyere – and I formed a new crew called UMA – which stood for Ultra Mega Awesome . . . 'The Ultra Mega Awesome Medley Of Wicked Cool Pow In Your Face Freestyle Stuff . . .' I can still remember it as if it was yesterday! It was kind of a weird name but it represented our personalities: we were just silly and energetic and loved having fun. We entered the UK Hip Hop Championships and came second, but once again a shortage of money meant we couldn't travel to the USA for our runners-up prize, which was gutting . . . again!

To be perfectly honest, my obsession with dancing really didn't help my studies. After GCSEs, I ended up only doing a year of sixth form because I didn't get good enough grades to carry on. I vividly remember the moment I got my poor results. I was like, *Ah, what are my parents going to say?* I wanted to make them proud so I was really bothered about the grades, even though I knew full well how it had happened. I owe a lot to my parents and I will always want to make them proud, so that was a difficult time. You want to make them happy as best you can, but at the same time you want to be happy yourself. It's just tricky sometimes trying to find the right balance.

This was made all the more difficult by my continued love of beatboxing, which I suppose seemed, from my parents' point of view, even more unlikely to earn me a living than dancing. Not that many people even know about beatboxing as an art form, to be honest. There also weren't many competitions or public platforms for beatboxing, so that hobby was slower to progress.

After my disappointing sixth form results, my sister suggested I look up the website of West Herts College in Watford. They had courses in business, catering, public services, loads of stuff that was useful, but I had no interest in those. Then I spotted a travel and tourism course that really appealed. I think travelling to Egypt so much as a kid had instilled in me a love of foreign cultures and globe-trotting. Although dancing was my number-one passion, I did want to prove to my parents that I could actually get some good grades. So for the next two years I knuckled down and ended up getting a double distinction — in fact, I loved the course so much that at the end of the final term I wanted to own a hotel!

'I wouldn't recommend being so distracted from your studies and I do regret it, but maybe that path wasn't meant for me. Maybe everything happens for a reason?'

When I hit eighteen, I entered loads more solo dance competitions, because I was no longer age-restricted from the clubs where they were held. At that age you win prize money, rather than just a trophy, so it was good to start earning a little money. I also started to teach dance, so there was the beginnings of an income, even if it was pretty modest. I noticed a big step up in the standard in the over-18s comps though, and I realized that I was going to have to train a lot harder, because these people had been doing this for years and had a lot more experience than I did. The first few times, I didn't get through pre-selections, I never even made it into the battle stages. That was frustrating, because I had gone from winning under-18s events to playing in the big-boy league and finding the leap in standard very challenging. It was really annoying, but I approached it like I do every other challenge – with hard work and yet more training.

After college, I ended up getting into Westminster University to study tourism with planning, which is essentially focused on the architecture side of the travel industry, how to develop a tourist destination and all that. This coincided with the first year that my dancing started to go really well: I was teaching regularly and making money, I was winning quite a few high-profile competitions, getting pretty well-known on the scene, really gathering momentum. Problem was, that took away from my concentration at uni for the whole of the first year and, being completely honest, I pretty much didn't attend classes. Looking back on it, that was really bad, but I was just so wrapped up in dancing and it was going so well. I wouldn't recommend being so distracted from your studies and I do regret it, but maybe that path wasn't meant for me. Maybe everything happens for a reason?

THE EARLY DAYS

JAM: So as you have seen, by this point in our story, we all knew of each other, we'd hung around town, played sport with and against each other, we'd even been in those few home-made recording studios at various times and in numerous combinations. But there was never anything formal, there was never a point where one of us said, 'This is great, let's form a band.'

Just after Ash and I got back from uni, I bumped into him at a party. We chatted and caught up with what we'd each been doing and I guess at some point during the evening I was singing and humming along to the music they were playing. Then Ash said, 'Jam, you can sing, man. We should record a few bits and pieces.' I liked the idea, and obviously Ash is a great guy.

ASH: His singing at that party was sick! I asked him if I could hear something that he'd recorded and I was amazed when he said he'd never used a professional studio before. To me, having been recording music since around the age of fifteen, it seemed crazy that someone who could sing like Jam hadn't ever been in a proper studio. Jamaal was very much in the same headspace as me, because he had been singing for forever but had never tried to do anything really focused with that talent. This coincided with my transition out of those difficult times at uni, when I just decided to really go for it. I was hell-bent on achieving!

JAM: The week after the party, I went to Ash's house and we wrote and then recorded a song called 'Roses', just like that. We were in his living room, and he plugged his iPhone headphones into his laptop and recorded me singing the melody; we came up with the words fairly organically. It was really fun and happened very naturally. That in itself was quite surprising to me, because apart from 'Find Your Love' way back in school, I hadn't written anything else, I hadn't studied songwriting, I hadn't been in any bands, but with Ash it just came so easily. Growing up, I'd only seen Ash now and then, some weeks more than others, but from that moment on I spoke to him literally every single day.

ASH: I believe that part of the reason we just clicked doing that song was that Jamaal didn't really listen to grime at all, he was from a completely different school of thought altogether. That seemed to inject a fresh approach into what I was thinking and the chemistry was just so immediate and productive. After that we decided we both felt suitably motivated to pay some money and go into a professional studio to record 'Roses' properly.

JAM: Ash knew of a local studio, so we hired that for a day and went in to record our song. That was a great experience because in a studio you have to be much more precise and technical. I wouldn't say I was naive about the process but it was certainly an eye-opener.

After that we were just writing songs all the time and almost recording them for the sake of it – we were really motivated. For example, there was a music platform that Ash introduced me to called Soulection; he was like, 'Jam, have you heard these beats? What do you think?' Well, they blew me away and we wrote some lyrics and melodies for those beats really quickly. We spent hours scouring SoundCloud and YouTube for great beats and inspiration. At that stage, we tended to write songs quite separate to each other. I always suggested to Ash that we should write together but he wasn't a fan of that, so we used to write separately and then bring the ideas together – and somehow it all just blended seamlessly and worked.

'It's one thing recording songs that you have written with each other in a studio, but to go up onstage in front of people, to put yourself out there like that, that's another level . . .'

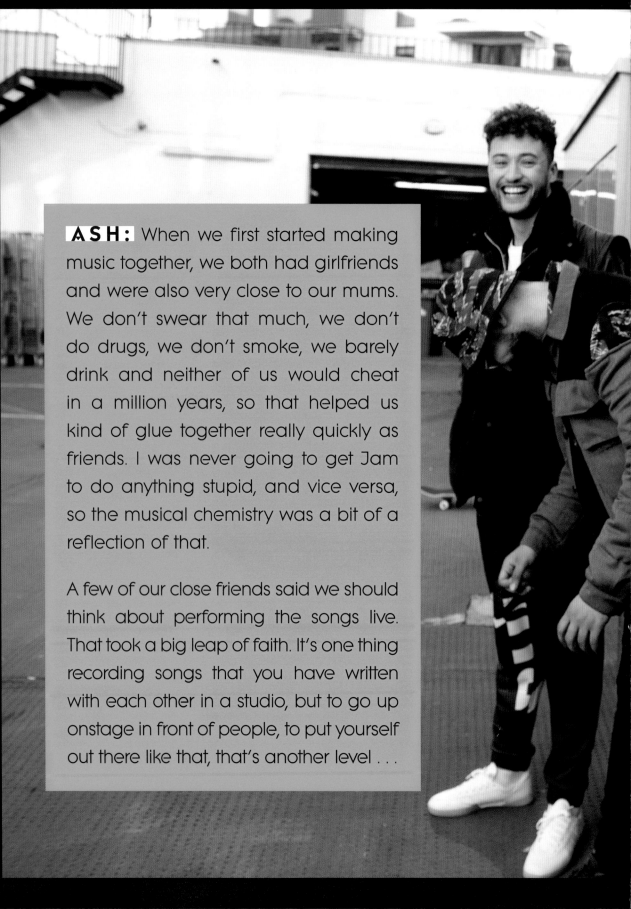

ASH: When we first started making music together, we both had girlfriends and were also very close to our mums. We don't swear that much, we don't do drugs, we don't smoke, we barely drink and neither of us would cheat in a million years, so that helped us kind of glue together really quickly as friends. I was never going to get Jam to do anything stupid, and vice versa, so the musical chemistry was a bit of a reflection of that.

A few of our close friends said we should think about performing the songs live. That took a big leap of faith. It's one thing recording songs that you have written with each other in a studio, but to go up onstage in front of people, to put yourself out there like that, that's another level . . .

JAM: You're not kidding. Do you remember the first gig we ever did together?

ASH: Middlesex Uni!

JAM: Exactly! We performed 'Roses' and another song called 'Which Way?' but we just stood there, holding the mics, not really moving at all! We were trying in our own way to get the crowd to vibe with us, but we didn't really know what we were doing. We just wanted to see what the music felt like to perform live, which meant that we didn't really think about how people were being entertained. I guess that is all part of the process of learning about performance. Some of our friends came down to support us, including Myles and Mus, who weren't yet involved in the music we were making.

MUS: I remember the sound system at Middlesex University had problems so the music wasn't as loud as it should have been; it just wasn't a great set-up. Jamaal was trying to get people to clap and a few were, but they were clapping out of time because they couldn't hear the track properly. Then Ash was trying to rap over the track, but that was tricky because of all the off-beat clapping, so I remember at one point him actually telling everyone to stop clapping! I think they started that song again. I definitely took the mickey out of him afterwards!

I've always been honest with them whenever they've asked my opinion and, to be frank, that debut performance was pretty static. In small venues like that it can be really hard work to get a crowd involved and grab their attention, so to be fair it was a pretty tricky first gig.

ASH: You're not kidding, Mus! Also it didn't really help that the early music (which eventually ended up on our first EP) was quite reflective and introverted, so it didn't make for a very good live spectacle. I guess if I was being harsh, I'd say the debut gig was a little boring.

Anyway, we were undeterred and after that first show we worked pretty hard actually, gigging sometimes twice a week. Remember, we were also playing basketball and football respectively to a high standard, so several nights a week we'd be busy training. Whenever there was a free night, we'd literally just type in 'R&B gigs' or 'open-mic nights' into Google and go somewhere and perform. On more than one occasion we caught the train into London and walked around until we found somewhere to perform.

'The problem was, as Ash says, it was getting to be an impossible balance. There just weren't enough hours in the day and there was a danger that we would spread ourselves too thin and end up underachieving at everything.'

JAM: The problem was, as Ash says, it was getting to be an impossible balance. There just weren't enough hours in the day and there was a danger that we would spread ourselves too thin and end up underachieving at everything.

I started to find that basketball was taking too much away from the music; getting to the fixtures sometimes took ages, and then, due to a big influx of new players, I was increasingly being left on the bench and not actually getting much game time. I felt I was past the age of really pushing to go out and play professionally in a different country and it felt like the momentum had stalled. I began to sense that I could get further with my music but that basketball was stifling that. I started to see basketball as more of a hobby and music as a passion that might evolve into something more . . . that said, for both of us to come away from a potential career in sport, which we had both dreamt of since we were little kids, was a big deal. However, the music was becoming something of an obsession, and we felt there was a chemistry in our writing and we loved performing. Over a period of time, I came to the conclusion that I wanted to prioritize music, which would mean I'd have to give up basketball as a career path but still play it as a hobby. For Ash, that same decision was very difficult because he was doing so well with his football.

ASH: Thanks, Jam! Yes, my football was going pretty well but by definition that meant a considerable time commitment. For example, I played one game in the FA Cup for Chesham United FC, and that meant I couldn't make a performance with Jam that night – I think in the end Mus went along with him. However, as Jam says, it was a big deal to come away from football. After uni, I'd made the decision to really focus and do everything to the best of my ability, but it was becoming impossible to juggle everything. So we started to have these discussions about making music our number-one priority. I remember Jam was all for it, he was positive and up for it. For a while, to be honest, I was still unsure, so I said, 'Are you *certain* you want to go through with this, Jam? You're absolutely sure?' It wasn't that I didn't want to, but I was always sceptical about putting myself out there. With music there are just a lot of intangibles and I also knew it was going to be a lot of work. I vividly remember having a long conversation; we sat in Jamaal's car around the corner from his house one night and we discussed the next step.

My main issue was that if we were going to prioritize the music, then we had to put *everything* into it. I was not prepared for this to be a 'one foot in' scenario, it was all or nothing. I needed to know Jam felt the same, because the last thing I wanted was for me to be in it whole-heartedly and for someone else to be half-hearted. Thankfully, with Jam that was never going to happen.

JAM: We agreed to go 100 per cent and put music above all else. That was a big decision! I was saying to him, 'Look, man, this is the first time I've ever done this. I'm trying to convince you that it will definitely work but I can't show you with anything else apart from my belief.' I think my naivety helped push us on, while Ash's realism helped rein us in and kept us grafting hard every day. It was just a really powerful balance.

Looking back, that day was the birth trigger for our first, independently released EP, *Flights 'n' Feels*. At that point it was still just myself and Ash, in terms of the actual writing. That debut EP was essentially just emotional music; you had to sit down and really take in what we were trying to say. That EP was great fun to make because it was something we found we could tap into quite easily, there was no struggle. I think that was because we weren't saying anything that we didn't believe in.

ASH: Our headspace for *Flights 'n' Feels* was that we both wanted to produce a body of work that we were going to be proud of, that's where the motivation came for it. The material we delved into was often from producers who were mostly in America, so that meant I had to research how you lease beats and how that side of the industry works. It was fascinating. Then I had to find us a decent studio, look into the money, do it all correctly. Once we were in the studio, we learnt so much about engineering and producing, then afterwards I had to look into releasing it independently and so on. We wanted to put out a few videos for key tracks – we did one for a song called 'Crystal Sky', for example. One of the videos was a little story acted out by my little brother and one of his friends – that needed researching, too. I guess in a way we were treating making music as a profession, even though it wasn't actually our job yet. Having Jam around was good; he helped me keep hold of my sanity, because he is always a little bit more laid-back and flexible.

I'm feeling you

I'm feeling you
So what we gonna do
I'm feeling you
So what we gonna do tonight
I'm feeling you
So what we gonna do
Yeah
I'm feeling you
So what we gonna do tonight

With the *Flights 'n' Feels* EP, we'd created a deeply introspective and therapeutic record – every word written across the seven songs meant something to us. Five of them are me and Jamaal together, one of them was an R&B song that Jam sang by himself and one of them was a spoken word track by me. Every single word on there was 100 per cent true. It is just me and Jamaal touching on things that we wouldn't necessarily talk about in person. He spoke about his girlfriend; we both talked about life in general; one song touched on university; another was a letter to my younger self. We took our time and really thought about the music and words, and at the end of the recording we were both really happy with what we had created.

> '**With the *Flights 'n' Feels* EP, we'd created a deeply introspective and therapeutic record – every word written across the seven songs meant something to us.'**

JAM: Those sessions were really enjoyable and, like Ash says, we learnt so much. Mus and Myles would pop into the studio to support us sometimes, so even though they weren't on the record itself, they were always around.

ASH: When we were writing for *Flights 'n' Feels*, we often used a little computer room upstairs at my house, usually me, Jamaal and Myles. He was helping us write, because he had always been there from the start and was a close friend. Obviously I knew Myles wrote his own stuff, and we had been recording songs with each other on and off over the years, so he was just always a part of what was going on. Mus was often there, too, even though he wasn't yet involved in the music.

MYLES: As you now know, I'd been writing lyrics for years but still wasn't actively making music with the boys. My football was going really well but when Ash came back from uni, I started to get more involved with music again. He would send me all these freestyles that he had written, but although I would frequently go to the studio with him throughout this period, I wasn't actively recording. I'm just the type of guy that doesn't jump into something straight away, I will sit back and watch. I just liked being there, hanging with my mates, probably on my phone a lot of the time! But then during the sessions for *Flight 'n' Feels*, I did start to have a little input. I wasn't writing with them, but they'd ask me for an opinion and I'd offer my thoughts. Mus was coming along at the same time, too.

MUS: Having left uni after the first year, I was trying to make it as a dancer. My plan was to teach dance and compete, but also get a part-time job, because the first two options offer a pretty unpredictable income. So I got a regular part-time job at a bar called Vodka Revolutions, and over the course of a year I ended up doing their promotions, too. I really got into that and enjoyed it very much. My job was to try and convince people to come to the bar, maybe give them free shots or chat to them, whatever. It definitely helped build my confidence in speaking to people. I needed to get more hours though, so eventually I ended up moving to Oceana Watford to become a promoter there. I worked my way up, going from promoter to promotions supervisor and then promotions manager, within two years. When I put my mind to something, I can be really focused.

The downside was the very long and anti-social working hours. Consequently I didn't go to the studio with the boys as much, because my shifts were so long. At weekends you just wouldn't see me because I would be working so late. However, I would still go to support them and hang out whenever I could find time.

JAM: When we dropped the *Flight 'n' Feels* EP, we had our own launch party at a place called Twisted Monkey in Watford. This was all self-funded – people paid for tickets and bought the EP as well, and we had a target figure in our heads of sixty paying customers to break even. This is where Mus really came into his own, because as a brilliant promotions manager he was a natural at putting on an event like this. He knew everyone and, if I recall correctly, he even DJ'd that night as well!

MUS: I did, yes! I was in my element organizing that launch night, to be honest, Jam. I was like, 'Okay, cool, look, I'll take the reins!' I remember thinking, *What can we do . . . what kind of show can we put on for people?* We all knew of various other local performers we liked, so we lined up three other acts to perform on the night, plus UMA Crew.

About two weeks before, I remember Ashley saying, 'Mus, I don't think people are going to come. Let's just cancel it.' I was like, 'Ashley, trust me. I promise you this will work. I know what I am doing. All you have to do is turn up and I promise it will work.' When the night came, we had, I believe, eighty-three people, which I was delighted with! Ashley was happy, too. The night itself was really good fun. Lots of people bought the EP and it was so nice that all these friends and family were there to support us. People were clapping, dancing and having a good time – the energy was really good.

ASH: To be fair to you, Mus, you did a great job! And if I'm honest, me and Jam didn't help much. It was nice that everyone we knew in Watford had come out to support us and that's why we tried to make a big event of it.

JAM: We sold a good few dozen EPs on the night and eventually a couple of hundred copies in total. Okay, this wasn't a record that made waves in the music industry, but it was a good, solid start. I think on the night we managed to pull in about a grand, which was really helpful because the music was all self-funded, so we could put that money back into the pot. Ashley had a pretty good job and had been funding quite a bit of the music up to this point, so it was good to take that weight off his shoulders a little.

'Okay, this wasn't a record that made waves in the music industry, but it was a good, solid start. I think on the night we managed to pull in about a grand, which was really helpful because the music was all self-funded, so we could put that money back into the pot.'

ASH: You're not kidding!

MYLES: With *Flights 'n' Feels*, they smashed it. It was good, and people were talking about it locally. That EP built up a fair amount of traction because it was an interesting record and also because they put in a lot of time and effort. That was kind of how the whole project started gathering momentum . . .

ASH: There is a little diversion from the main story at this point. After *Flights 'n' Feels* but before Mus and Myles officially joined, me and Jam did a performance at a nearby university, and afterwards this Italian dude called Riccardo came up, said he was working on some music, looking for rappers to work with and would we be interested in collaborating. We swapped details and he did indeed send over some cool music. The subject matter wasn't really something that me and Jam were feeling because it was mostly about girls and partying (we both had girlfriends). However, to cut a long story short, fast-forward a couple of months and this guy invited us over to France to do a gig at a launch party he was holding.

We went out to this venue in Paris called the Cartel Club and it was just the coolest thing ever, the way everyone was dressed, the music, it was just so impressive. This guy and his friends had VIP tables and knew everyone, he was like a celebrity there. We were like, *What is going on? This is amazing!*

The gig was brilliant and we were treated really nicely, then the next day we wandered around Paris, had a bit of food, went to a studio and made some more music – it was just the best experience. All the time we were sending Mus and Myles photos and videos. Now, the point of telling all this is that it made us realize if we worked really hard on our music, our lives could be like this. Yes, we knew it wouldn't all be clubs and parties and seeing famous cities, we weren't naive enough to think that, but it was a taster, a flavour of what it could be like. For me, if there was a point in time when it switched from just doing music as a hobby to the seed being planted of actually thinking what this could be like as a career, going to Paris was that moment. That really spurred us on.

MUS: Meanwhile, back in Watford! Perhaps we should explain about the name . . .

JAM: Good point, Mus. So before the first EP came out, we were calling ourselves Tracks X Suits. The idea was to represent the duality of our lives – writing music and wearing tracksuits was where we wanted to be, but the reality of life was that we had to put on suits (metaphorically or actually) to pay the bills. 'Tracks' was the playful music side of our lives, 'Suits' was the work and job element. The problem was, people didn't really understand the name, they'd get confused and say, 'Is that Tracks versus Suits or is it X-Suits?' Other people called us Tracks-Suits or Track Times Suits – there was a lot of confusion, it just wasn't working. One day we all met up at Nando's to figure out a new name. Myles and Mus were there, as ever, and we sat down and came up with all these ideas. At one point Ash went to the loo, and on his way back he said, 'Guys, why don't we just shorten the name to Rak-Su?'

'It just had a ring to it and there wasn't any confusion, it was just a cool-sounding name. We mentioned it to one of Mus's managers at a local venue and he said it sounded cool . . . so that was that: Rak-Su.'

ASH: It just had a ring to it and there wasn't any confusion, it was just a cool-sounding name. We mentioned it to one of Mus's managers at a local venue and he said it sounded cool . . . so that was that: Rak-Su.

JAM: At this point, my basketball helped us a little, getting us what would prove to be Mus's first official gig with us. The coach who had been trying to set me up to play in Gran Canaria also held a basketball fun day on the south coast during the annual Brighton Summer Madness event, and in the summer of 2016 he asked us if we'd like to go down there and perform. At the time, we felt our performance needed to be boosted somehow. Maybe it was the introspective style of music, perhaps it was our relative lack of experience, but we all agreed it needed something extra. We also all knew about Mus's long and successful history of dance competitions . . .

MUS: The problem was that they were required to do a twenty-minute set but they didn't have enough material for that. So it was suggested that I go along and do some cover songs with Jam. They also had a song called 'Dragon' and I really liked the beat behind that, so I said I'd be able to dance to that, too.

ASH: Brighton was our first big gig. By 'big' I mean in front of more than fifteen people! There were probably still only about fifty people on the beach and, to be honest, a lot of them weren't even paying attention! But it felt like a big moment, mostly because Mus was there with us onstage.

MUS: Not sure I'd call it a stage, to be fair! Even so, the reaction we got was really good! It was a real buzz, actually.

JAM: When it came to 'Dragon', it was almost like Mus was spitting flames on that section of the track . . . it was probably one of our favourite songs to perform because it was so energetic. Mus was amazing that day!

MYLES: I was always there, supporting them, literally just standing in the crowd, being a friend. I wasn't inclined to join in officially, to be honest. I enjoyed writing my music and supporting them with theirs. Mus certainly knew how to perform, he brought something different to the table. He brought his beatbox in and he would do his dancing and it really lifted the whole vibe.

JAM: On the drive home after the Brighton gig, I said to Mus, 'That felt really good! Is this something that you'd want to be involved in more permanently?' and he said, 'Absolutely!'

ASH: We all really enjoyed that gig, and Myles thought it was cool, too. After that we wanted to make the most of the fact we now had a twenty-minute set, so we started to book up more shows with Mus. We did a gig at the prestigious Notting Hill Arts Club, which incorporated even more of his beatboxing, and it felt like our performance was improving with every show.

JAM: Do you remember, Ash, you created a narrative to accompany the songs at that show? And you pulled someone out of the crowd! You added a story to every song and the crowd seemed to really enjoy it. I felt that night, certainly in terms of confidence onstage, we began taking our performance to another level. We started to shape how we wanted to perform and the roles for each member.

ASH: Then it got to a point where we started writing a couple of songs specifically because they were the right sort of sound that Mustafa could dance to, which we knew would enhance the live experience even more.

MYLES: I was watching these gigs and hanging around in the studio, having banter with them, but all the time I was also writing my own material. My football was going well, I was getting paid for it, training hard, playing well. However, I was also at an age when, realistically, time was beginning to run out. Soccer is a very young game and by my early twenties I'd started to think, *I'm not going*

'However, I was also at an age when, realistically, time was beginning to run out. Soccer is a very young game and by my early twenties I'd started to think, *I'm not going to make it as a professional footballer.*'

___

to make it as a professional footballer. I realized it wasn't going to happen at the highest level. My little brother plays for Watford, so I was happy seeing him do well and kind of live my dream of football through him. I had a good job working for Ash's mum at the nursing agency, so that was bringing in decent money, too.

Around the time of their debut EP, I wrote a song called 'C'est La Vie' about a French girl I was seeing. When I showed it to the lads, they absolutely loved it. They knew I was writing, and Ashley had always respected me as an MC – he loves my flow and production style – so it was nice to have them say such complimentary things about my material.

ASH: I loved this tune and really wanted to jump on it and work with Myles. Jamaal felt the same, we all loved it. We ended up recording that tune and that's how Myles became more actively involved in the group. He was always at the studio and came to every gig anyway, so we were like, 'Stop being an idiot and get involved!'

MYLES: I was happy to become more involved at that point but it still wasn't anything official just yet. Not long after they recorded 'C'est La Vie' with me, they had a gig down in Brixton and I went along to support them. After the show we had a massive discussion about where the band was going.

JAM: We all had decent jobs and the band was costing us money; there was football and various other career paths set out – essentially we'd come to a fork in the road. After the Brixton show, we were all pretty tired and fed up, and we ended up on a street corner having a heated discussion . . .

ASH: I'd say argument . . .

JAM: Okay, we ended up having an argument about the future of the band.

MYLES: I remember that well! There we were, arguing on a street corner in the middle of Brixton at two in the morning, freezing cold, proper sketchy. I was tired, I had work at six and they were having a full-blown argument.

ASH: We started to put the heat on Myles until finally one of us just said, 'Look, Myles, if we go for it, are you going to get involved in this?' As you know, he is very laid-back and so in classic Myles-style, he just raised his eyebrows and said, 'Yeah, okay, cool.' So that was that: Rak-Su was now a four-piece.

JAM: Me, Mus and Ash were this collective before Myles stepped on to the scene, but when he formally joined, he pretty much added the crucial final element we needed to take things to a different level, to take the band up a gear, to add a little bit more colour to the palette. He wanted to do more up-tempo music, too – there is a fun, skippy side to Myles and a more mellow, methodical side to Ashley, so it balanced up quite nicely. Myles just seemed to fit in immediately.

ASH: For me, that set the wheels in motion. I was like, *Ah, actually, I can see this going somewhere else now.* I started to plan a whole bunch of new stuff because suddenly, in my head at least, we had a route. Myles kind of injected a whole lot of fun. We started gigging with him, although to be fair it took a little while for Myles to find his legs performance-wise because he was quite shy; he would perform almost with his chin on his chest! However, once he overcame that it started to really, really work. In terms of live shows, after Myles joined we felt that we were really improving, there was more of a dynamic and we were starting to understand how to put on a show. That said, it wasn't always plain sailing.

'People would sometimes say that our music didn't fit in anywhere, that our line-up was too unusual – why didn't we have more singers, why did we have a dancer and a guy who did beatbox? It was hard to make it clear to some people how we worked.'

MYLES: To a degree, some of the issues with how we were received were due to our unusual line-up. It's not conventional to have two guys rapping, one beatboxing or dancing, and one singing. That's not how traditional 'boy' or 'man' bands work. Sometimes we'd be booked for a pop gig and there'd be too much rapping for that audience, plus we were four big guys, two of whom had previously been heavily into grime. There were other times when we'd play a more urban venue and there'd be too much pop for that crowd, and not enough grime or rap.

We never got a look in at any record label; we got widely rejected from music sites such as SubmitHub and places like that. People would sometimes say that our music didn't fit in anywhere, that our line-up was too unusual – why didn't we have more singers, why did we have a dancer and a guy who did beatbox? It was hard to make it clear to some people how we worked. It was a dilemma but we just had to persevere, to keep true to our sound and the vision of how we saw the band moving forward. Sometimes we would do well, sometimes we didn't – one particular performance in Dalston was an example of where we didn't deal with it very well.

JAM: Oh, jeez, Dalston. Who wants to tell this story?

MUS: I will take this one for the team! So, we did this performance as a four-piece at a rooftop garden in east London. The other artists were good performers, they were super-self-assured, very polished and serious, and they all went down really well. By contrast, our set was fun and light-hearted, but that wasn't what the crowd were looking for. The audience just all sat around the edge of the rooftop looking completely unimpressed.

'I remember trying to find the positive in what she had said, but I couldn't see anything, not one scrap of good news, which is unusual for me.'

ASH: It was horrible. We just melted because we didn't get any energy back from the crowd; that meant we stopped putting the good energy out so we were half-hearted, it was a really awkward performance and I was just waiting for it to end. Then this guy called J Flows came on after us and the whole place was instantly rocking!

MUS: Although the crowd was quite quiet and it was fairly hard work to get any energy out of them, it wasn't a disaster, in my view. However, there was a woman watching who was very experienced in the music industry, and after the gig we asked her opinion and she completely destroyed us! She just ripped us apart. She said Jamaal had an amazing voice and could do it on his own; she told us that Myles didn't have any confidence onstage and we didn't need him; she questioned why a dancer/beatboxer was onstage at all; and she questioned Ash's presence, too. Not the greatest review! The most painful part was that she really knew her stuff, and so we had to respect her opinion. She was very polite but very clear – for her, it didn't work at all.

ASH: We got in the car to drive back to Watford together and had never been so flat. Everyone was kind of broken. I remember trying to find the positive in what she had said, but I couldn't see anything, not one scrap of good news, which is unusual for me. I was mostly worried about Myles, because he didn't say a word the entire drive back. I was really concerned about how he was taking it.

MUS: We were absolutely gutted, completely disheartened. It was pretty hard to feel positive about the feedback but gradually we picked over what she had said and realized there was a lot of substance in her criticism and that we simply needed to work and work and work to improve. We knew that we were very unconventional. We are not a typical boy band. But those comments cut us up really badly.

'Most importantly of all, that night made us more determined than ever to make it work. From that moment on we were like, *Right, let's rehearse constantly, prep every show, look at how we present ourselves onstage and on social media, think about our next studio work, basically look into every detail of this group. Let's make this happen.*'

————————

ASH: Then the next day, an amazing thing happened. Myles sent a message in a group chat about a song that we were working on. He didn't mention the night before, there was no negativity or feeling sorry for himself, he was just cracking on. It was such an incredible way to react.

MUS: After Dalston, we all just decided to knuckle down and make this work even more. Firstly we had a big conversation about the dynamics onstage, about how to boost Myles's confidence, about blending all the elements together. We really stood back and reassessed what we were doing. Most importantly of all, that night made us more determined than ever to make it work. From that moment on we were like, *Right, let's rehearse constantly, prep every show, look at how we present ourselves onstage and on social media, think about our next studio work, basically look into every detail of this group. Let's make this happen.*

JAM: We set up loads of WhatsApp groups for every different element of Rak-Su so that we could keep all this discussion organized and flowing, it was a massive amount of work and energy, especially as we were all still in demanding full-time jobs.

We started to look within our performance, at what we could do to (1) never feel that way again, and (2) make sure we took away positives and evolved as a result. There weren't actually any drastic changes; no one was saying that the music was crap, just that our material wasn't performed as well as it could be. Part of that was the tone of the music, which we all knew was relatively mellow. There wasn't that much that we could really get the crowd involved in, and if you are turning up to venues with people paying for tickets, obviously you want to be able to draw them in to the performance in some way.

ASH: The next performance we did was a million miles better and, to be honest, we never, ever looked back. That Dalston lady slating us made us realize we actually had a long way to go. From that moment on our performances just jumped up. I actually saw that lady recently and thanked her for giving us that wake-up call. She hadn't intended to upset us but there was no point asking for her opinion if we were just going to ignore someone so experienced. Looking back, Dalston was a watershed moment because after that we really raised our game.

'We started to look within our performance, at what we could do to (1) never feel that way again, and (2) make sure we took away positives and evolved as a result.'

MYLES: Throughout this period, it was just constant writing, writing, writing songs. We soon had over sixty songs recorded, and to complement that we were performing relentlessly, getting our name about, literally up and down the UK. It cost so much money – we were pumping thousands of pounds into the band – but that's what we all wanted to do.

I would say that this momentum was driven by Ashley, the majority of it, anyway. Ash is very structured; he usually knows what to do and if he doesn't know, he'll buy a book about it and teach himself. Anyway, over a quite short space of time we had so many songs that we needed to start thinking about our next release . . .

Ashley always says it was a breath of fresh air when I joined because I brought a different style of music that was upbeat, hyped, bubbly. We all agreed that the music needed to be more upbeat, and it was out of these discussions that 'I'm Feeling You' was born, from an idea of Jam's, and it became the first song we completed as a four-piece.

JAM: We had been back to the studio to try a few ideas and one of these was this chorus and verse I'd written. I sent that to Ash and asked him what he thought . . .

ASH: I loved it . . . I told him I thought it was sick.

JAM: So we worked on that and it gradually evolved into 'I'm Feeling You'; unknown to us at the time, it was a song that would change all of our lives.

'Throughout this period, it was just constant writing, writing, writing songs. We soon had over sixty songs recorded, and to complement that we were performing relentlessly, getting our name about, literally up and down the UK.'

choose what to see though, I'll meet you at heathrow
Pick a destination Maldives or Montego-
Bay lets hit Hawaii, Abu Dhabi or Dubai
lets listen to phil collins & be in the air tonight

It was fate not by mistake she fell in love wit dahkid
Her shape is great a burning flame she burning bright like a wick
English, Cuban, Jamaican she so in love wit the mix
So I took her 2 Jamaica slap some patois pon it

and now we, ride round inna di soft top
ah Seah mi tun and yuh aatt di gyal ah love dat-
watteh me so yuh know mi affi watch back
whats appen a she gunna chat back

MUS: We had some songs that Ash and Jam had previously written, but now they were revisited and Myles started putting his lyrical touch on them. We gradually built up this new catalogue of material that was sounding much more upbeat, a definite progression from *Flights 'n' Feels*. That was how we started to write the second EP, which would simply be called *Dive*.

MYLES: There was definite progression in this period. The writing process had evolved noticeably and we knew very clearly what each one of us brought to the table. We all have different elements. Jamaal is an emotional guy, he thinks with his heart. Ashley is the brains; he likes structure, he likes having a storyline. For me, as long as a song is upbeat then I can bring my personality to the tune; I'll make sure I'm getting seventeen syllables a bar or I'll come with a skippy flow that just entices people and excites their minds. And Mus has the twin gifts of beatboxing and dancing to make it very visual. In my opinion, it works perfectly. We know exactly what we want out of each other and exactly how to get that.

MUS: There were probably about nine songs that had the potential to be on the second EP. We played all of these to various friends and no one said they disliked a single song. And our friends have always been honest, they know it's pointless just saying everything is brilliant if they don't feel that. So that was a boost — we knew that we had made a step up in terms of new material. Everyone really liked 'I'm Feeling You', but there were other songs that generated a lot of interest, such as 'Dive' and 'All Day Long'.

ASH: For the second EP, we used exactly the same process as before: YouTube, SoundCloud, trawling through beats online, finding all these inspirational sounds. One of us would make a playlist and send it out to all the other guys, they might add something or change a part, and over time these new songs began taking shape. Our writing process had become a little more collaborative, incredibly fluid and natural, so it felt fun as well. There has never been one main writer in Rak-Su. Every song is initially spearheaded by an individual, then we all contribute and work out the final version. Of course, sometimes someone might not like a sound or song, but because we have all been friends forever they can make that point without anyone taking offence. We spend a lot of time with each other so we just say it how it is, 100 per cent honest. We never had egos to start with, and we'd spent too much time with each other and knew each other too well to have any of that; it would not be tolerated.

MYLES: Day in, day out. I will tell the boys if their music is rubbish! Just before I was working on this chapter, I did it to Ashley on the tour bus. He played me a new song and I said, 'Yeah, the chorus is good, but your verse is absolutely terrible!' We get annoyed for about five minutes and then just decide to write something better.

ASH: For the *Dive* EP we wanted to have every song completely sorted before we stepped into a studio, because we would be paying by the hour so we couldn't afford to be experimenting with music while the clock was running. It worked really well and we ended up creating music that had a lot more energy to it, a lot more of a vibe. It was much more fun to perform and consequently more people took notice.

MYLES: The *Dive* EP came out in April 2017, released independently by us.

MUS: Stepping up from the previous record, we had both a listening party and a launch party to kick this record off, which obviously I organized using my promoter contacts and experience. The listening party was a free event and we invited tons of people that we knew, local music-scene faces, friends, family and musicians – it was a great mix. A lot of these people had been supporting our musical journey so it was an ideal opportunity to get them all in the same room listening to our new material. We held it in the downstairs area of a place called Gabriel's in Watford, which did food as well, and people seemed to really enjoy the night.

Then we had the actual launch party at a bar called Faborjé in Watford, and again I did all the promotion side of it, the flyers, organizing the support acts, trying to fill the venue and make it a great night for everyone. It's a lot of work! Promoting a night club is easy by comparison, because people are already out to have good time, but to get people to come and support an unsigned, relatively unknown group and spend their hard-earned money is a much harder task. The second EP launch was a much more efficient set-up: we had lanyards, USBs, merchandise and flyers. It was really professional.

As it happened, we had a great turnout and eventually counted over two hundred people on the night, which was pretty amazing. There was a really good vibe all evening and people said they loved the songs. That was probably one of the best nights where I felt that I had achieved something. For me, from the first EP to the second there was a significant progression: musically, performance-wise, the organization, our profile, everything about it was a step up.

'For me, from the first EP to the second there was a significant progression: musically, performance-wise, the organization, our profile, everything about it was a step up.'

JAM: Commercially the second EP did a lot better, there were more people listening to it and more people bought it. Okay, it still wasn't a massive mainstream hit – we didn't even have a record deal, remember – but people were increasingly getting into the band.

MYLES: Watford was now behind us, we were making a lot of noise in the local area and people were coming to our gigs to show their support. It wasn't just friends and family either, it was people who had just somehow heard of Rak-Su. A small indication of that was we started selling a lot of our Rak-Su hats, which actually became a source of income.

MUS: We made a decent amount of money from that launch night and I remember saying to Ashley, 'Let's put all of that money into Rak-Su, let's use it for more videos, more studio time, buy more beats. Let's make this work.' At that time I needed my share of the money for myself as I wasn't earning much. But I knew that was the wrong thing to do. We had to pump every penny back into the band.

ASH: We would send out our songs to literally all of the music blogs that we could think of, all of the YouTube channels, anyone and anywhere to try and get them to support us. We spent days and weeks and months on end, sitting at a laptop, scouring the internet for ways to get our music out there.

MUS: We were also posting all the time on YouTube, Instagram, Facebook, videos, photos, news updates . . . we were always putting content online. The whole period proved we were actually growing as a band. Some of the videos were just me and Jam doing these medleys: he'd be singing and I'd beatbox. We posted a few of those and they were getting 50, 60, 80,000 views. We mashed up artists such as Nickelback, the Script and Oasis, it was a little bit different. We even did a Disney medley! We were just trying to find out loads of different and interesting ways of being able to promote ourselves and get known.

JAM: We'd started to get more positive responses, so the ball was rolling. We were doing great performances and people were starting to really, really like us and buy into us. We got played on 'BBC Introducing' a couple of times, then a woman called Jamz Supernova played one of our songs on 1Xtra, and we had been on local radio, too. It was definitely progressing.

Our onstage presence had improved so much as well. One of our favourite things to do is the band call-and-response, when we say to the crowd, 'Rak what?' and the audience shouts back, 'Rak-Su!' Of course, you have to be pretty confident that they will respond, otherwise you'll look very stupid! It wasn't every night that we could try that, but when it worked, that was a real buzz. There were some great gigs around this time.

ASH: Certainly were. Remember Aldershot? That was unreal. It was an under-18s disco. They printed up this flyer with our name on it and when we got to this town hall, and it was the first time that we had an actual dressing room! We were buzzing, especially when we found out there was a PlayStation in there! It was a proper stage, we got paid a couple of hundred pounds for it as well, and there were 300 kids dancing and having a great time. Afterwards they even had us do a little signing – it was such a good night, a real boost.

During this time we also learnt that regardless of the gig and the atmosphere, our performance should *never* drop. We always perform as if there are 1,000 people in front of us having the best time of their lives. That was a really important realization.

MYLES: At another gig in Guildford we were given a roped-off VIP area, which made us feel special, even though we were too self-conscious to use it! We did a mini festival in Watford, loads of club gigs. We were working in the day, still doing our sport and then every spare second we were gigging, gigging, gigging. It felt like something was starting to happen . . .

ASH: At the same time, there was a problem. We were all juggling way too much. I was still playing football at a semi-pro level, and so was Myles. Jam was working hard and Mus had his night-shift work in promotions. We had our training, bills to pay, recording, gigging. I don't think any of us got much sleep and some nights we'd get in late, crash into bed and be up early the next morning to start all over again. It couldn't carry on, something had to give. Then I missed a performance – I couldn't get there because I had a cup game that went to extra time, and Jamaal and Mus got really annoyed with me. I understood that, but it wasn't possible to carry on doing everything any more. We all had decisions to make.

JAM: It was coming to the point where we were going to have to give ourselves an ultimatum, to choose one path over the others: Rak-Su, football or our professional careers. Myles had pushed that decision back a little bit when he joined but the dilemma was still there. I'd also been accepted for a master's degree course, which was amazing; Myles and Ash were playing serious football; Mus had finally jumped ship from his nightlife work and started a career in the hotel industry, which he had always wanted to do – all of this on top of the band, which in itself was enough work for four guys every day. Rak-Su had evolved from a hobby into a passion into a cool local band, and now our progress was really quite significant. We ran the risk of underachieving at everything by trying to do too much. Plus at some point the money was going to run out . . . something had to be done. It was time to go all or nothing . . .

ASH: Ultimately I made the momentous decision to walk away from football. I'd been playing since I was eight and to be a professional had been a lifelong dream of mine, but I realized I wanted to pursue music more. That's why I made that call. So did everyone else. Jamaal declined the masters, something he had been striving to achieve for years, and Myles also pulled away from football.

MYLES: I did, I stepped away from football, which was paying me well, to concentrate on the band, which was costing us a fortune. However, we just all knew what needed to be done. It was time to put all our eggs in one basket.

MUS: I wanted to leave nightlife because I didn't feel that it was healthy for me. I was really good at my job but I couldn't see myself doing it for the rest of my life. It got to the point where I just wasn't enjoying it any more, but I knew that Rak-Su was there and that was what I couldn't stop thinking about. To be honest, in some ways I was struggling for a direction, I didn't know which path to follow, but the one thing that always energized and excited me was the band.

'Leading up to this show, we had actually been approached by talent scouts for both *The X Factor* and *The Voice*, asking us to consider auditioning. They were all saying, "Look, guys, we think you are talented. It would be quite cool if you came down to the show, tried out, see how it goes. If you don't like it, then at least you've given it a go."'

JAM: Then came a gig at a gay bar called Freedom in central London, a night that changed *everything* for us. Leading up to this show, we had actually been approached by talent scouts for both *The X Factor* and *The Voice*, asking us to consider auditioning. They were all saying, 'Look, guys, we think you are talented. It would be quite cool if you came down to the show, tried out, see how it goes. If you don't like it, then at least you've given it a go.' There was never any pressure there. However, at that point, it wasn't what we wanted to do. We were happy putting our music out independently and, to be brutally honest, some of us had reservations about doing a TV talent show and whether that would suit our band and our music.

ASH: Anyway, we had this gig booked at Freedom. We'd never performed in that area of London before so we didn't know what to expect. We didn't even know if they had regular music nights or not, but we were always keen to gig and put our name out there.

MUS: I hadn't long started my new hotel job so I couldn't get any time off; it was still quite anti-social hours but at least I was working in an industry where I wanted to be. Unfortunately, this meant that I couldn't make the Freedom gig.

ASH: We travelled into London and made our way to the downstairs room of the club. Obviously the environment was completely alien to us – the whole place was pink and it was certainly a new experience! For some reason we were on last, so we sat down and watched some of the other acts and they were really, really good but super-poppy, nothing remotely urban at all. So, I was watching this and thinking, *I've got no idea how we are going to be received! This could be a disaster!*

JAM: Fortunately, when we went onstage, our performance was great fun and went down really well; the crowd was brilliant! We were having a laugh and a joke with each other and I think that resonated with the audience. It really helped that the acoustics were incredible, the whole set-up in there was great. Anyway, immediately afterwards this girl approached us and introduced herself as a talent scout, she said we were very good and really should consider going on *The X Factor*.

ASH: Initially, just as when we had been asked previously about those shows, we were a little bit apprehensive. However, for some reason, this time we felt slightly more open to the idea, I think perhaps because it wasn't the first time someone had said that to us, so we were beginning to wonder if there was something in it.

MYLES: After the Freedom gig, we sat and talked about the idea of going on *The X Factor*. We talked for ages, it was pretty intense. Let's be frank here – we had a big argument. If I remember rightly, Mustafa was totally against it. I think Jamaal was hesitant at the time. Ash was more intrigued, he thought it could work. And I was totally into it. I was the only person who said, 'A hundred per cent we have to do this.' Yes, it was a risk, but I felt it was a chance we had to take, that there was no point *not* doing it and then wondering what might have been. I had so much faith in our music, I knew we would do well or, at least, I knew a few people would like us.

'We sat and talked about the idea of going on *The X Factor*. We talked for ages, it was pretty intense. Let's be frank here –we had a big argument. If I remember rightly, Mustafa was totally against it. I think Jamaal was hesitant at the time. Ash was more intrigued, he thought it could work. And I was totally into it.'

JAM: I was worried about the stigma around TV talent shows – quite a lot of people are less than friendly towards acts from these programmes and often make judgements about the artists who do well on those shows. Also, I was worried that the acts that have come from *X Factor* hadn't been anything like us, in terms of writing all their own material and performing original songs on the show. Potentially worst of all, there were some people who went on the show and came away perceived as nothing more than a joke. It was a big risk. I was not convinced.

'My head was always in Rak-Su. So to dismiss the idea of going on the biggest music show in the country didn't seem to make sense to me. There were risks, yes, but there were a lot of advantages, too.'

ASH: For me personally, by this point I wanted us to get as far as possible. I really believed in our music, people seemed to really like our songs and took the time to listen to what we created. However, the harsh reality was that not enough people knew about us. Not enough people had heard us. We'd poured over ten grand and years of our lives into Rak-Su. I'd stopped playing football for this. My productivity at work was going down because I was always sat on the computer trying to figure out how we were going to get on to this music blog or planning a video or whatever. My head was always in Rak-Su. So to dismiss the idea of going on the biggest music show in the country didn't seem to make sense to me. There were risks, yes, but there were a lot of advantages, too. Imagine if we were filmed and they played our song on *one* show, if we were broadcast *once* to the country – imagine how helpful that would be. That was my position. For me, pragmatically speaking, it was an opportunity that might lead to something else – we kind of had to take it.

MUS: I was dead against it. Personally, I was scared of how we would be perceived because I didn't want the rooftop garden in Dalston to happen again but on a national, televised scale. I had serious reservations. We'd all watched *X Factor*, and you didn't really see any rappers or beatboxers on there. I was worried we'd just be seen as a weird, novelty act. I didn't want them to pick us apart on national TV. I was worried we could be *X Factor* rejects, that was all going through my mind. It seemed like the odds would be stacked against us. I don't think I was the only one with those concerns, but I was probably the most reluctant. I just said to the boys, 'If we are going to do this, let's showcase our own music, let's represent ourselves in a way that we will be proud of.'

ASH: The problem was that there wasn't a unanimous view in the band. That night after Freedom was a big crossroads, because for the first time we fought verbally, we dealt with some strongly conflicting views on the whole *X Factor* idea and everyone was pretty passionate.

Shortly after that pivotal evening, we had a gig booked at a food festival in a car park in Shoreditch, but when we got there, there was no PA, no stage, it was just a disaster. In fact, there was no practical way we would be able to perform so that was a downer, but what we did instead was decide to eat! We all went off and bought these enormous plates of food, sat around a bench and just chatted for ages about Rak-Su's future and, naturally, *The X Factor*. We drew up a list of things that we wanted to achieve, so for example the YouTube channels that we wanted to be on, the blogs we wanted to be covered by, the views we wanted to get, the number of SoundCloud plays we wanted to achieve, the live shows we wanted to play . . . everything you could think of. Then we said, 'Let's put a time limit on this.' The first audition for *The X Factor* was going to be in a couple of months' time, so I suggested if we could achieve our list of goals within that period of time completely by ourselves, then we didn't need the show. However, if the two months had gone by and we had not achieved the results we wanted, then I felt we should take the massive helping hand offered by appearing on one of the nation's biggest shows. And always, I was of the view that if we did do the show, we would do it on *our terms*, writing and performing our original music. There was consensus on that; none of us wanted to go on there and just perform covers.

'And always, I was of the view that if we did do the show, we would do it on *our terms*, writing and performing our original music. There was consensus on that; none of us wanted to go on there and just perform covers.'

MYLES: Meanwhile we were still gigging in and around Watford and London, still working away, trying to progress. After eight weeks or so we had achieved some of the targets we'd set but not all of them – we were making progress but not at the rate that a big TV show might generate. So, at the end of our two months' time limit, we had a band vote and the call was made: we were going to audition for *The X Factor*.

JAM: That night we all agreed that our target was to get on the televized auditions and perform 'I'm Feeling You' to the judges. That way our own song would be aired to millions of people across the UK. What an opportunity that would be. I remember thinking, *Wow, if we can just do that, if we can get to sing one of our own songs on a TV talent show, this whole X Factor experience could be a great stepping stone . . .*

MYLES: The question was, had we made the right decision?

THE X FACTOR

THE JOURNEY BEGINS . . .

'People always ask what that first audition day is like and I just say, "Filming and more filming and more filming!"

A S H : Before we did *The X Factor* audition, there was a small acoustic gig we performed that might seem insignificant on the surface but was actually a pivotal moment in the group's story. We were asked to do an acoustic festival, which was intriguing to us but at the same time pretty daunting. All of our performances so far had been to a backing track, with loudspeakers and high energy, so acoustic was totally out of our comfort zone. A friend of ours recommended this guitarist called Hus, who subsequently offered to figure out some material that would work acoustically; we were amazed when he turned up for rehearsals and had somehow turned our songs into these acoustic numbers that really worked! Very clever – we were just completely blown away. We played around with the riffs and the timing, tweaked a few melodies. It was really fascinating, a whole new way of looking at music.

Anyway, we did the acoustic festival and it seemed to go down pretty well. It was a relief but also completely exhilarating. Then we did a series of 'Sofa Sounds' gigs, where you go to people's houses and perform in their living rooms! This was all totally new to us, but the point I am trying to make is that relearning our material for an acoustic setting made us rethink everything we knew about music; we had to really understand each part and why the music did – or didn't – work. Later, when we were performing at various stages of *The X Factor*, that experience would prove absolutely crucial to us being able to progress.

MYLES: I was due to be in Jamaica on the day of the London filming of the *X Factor* televised auditions. Fortunately, we managed to figure out a way to attend the Manchester audition instead, although on the day we were due to travel up north we first had two other gigs down south – including one at Westfield Shopping Centre!

ASH: I remember that gig well! People weren't there to hear music, they were there to shop. We were performing as thousands of people just wandered past; sometimes they'd stop and listen, sometimes they'd stop and just be texting their mates or looking up where a certain shop was. But hey, that's what it's like. You have to put the hard yards in.

MUS: Leading up to the audition we were rehearsing for what seemed like twenty-four hours a day! We also had our little WhatsApp groups discussing loads of different ideas about how we wanted to look, and in the end we took two or three different outfits, just in case.

JAM: That was a long day . . . two gigs down south, then off up to Manchester . . .

MYLES: After those gigs, we drove up to Manchester and booked into an Airbnb. We stayed up till two a.m. rehearsing and having arguments about whether our outfits should match or not! In the end, we decided the clothes should be black or white, and I'm pretty sure we ended up sleeping in our outfits! The funny thing was, after we'd finished rehearsing, Mus and I weren't tired at all, so we headed out into Manchester to have a look around and find some clubs or whatever. I think we got back in pretty late, to be fair.

JAM: The audition was at the Old Trafford Cricket Ground and we had to be up early to start queuing at nine a.m – and remember, we had never been in an audition before, ever . . .

MUS: I hate queuing. I absolutely hate it . . .

JAM: Ha ha! Well, it was a pretty massive queue, wasn't it? There were thousands of people already there; it was quite a sight to see, actually.

ASH: And it was raining . . .

MYLES: After a while, though, they picked us out of the queue, guided us through these barriers and said, 'You guys have got a busy day.' We weren't really sure what they meant, to be honest. They started interviewing us on camera, then took loads of footage of us walking together, hanging out, all sorts. It was a very, very full-on day. We saw other acts getting picked out, too, so we were trying to guess what was going on.

JAM: People always ask what that first audition day is like and I just say, 'Filming and more filming and more filming!'

'There were certain points where our energy would dip and then we would have to try and perk ourselves back up again. As mates, that was easy; we were used to being around each other all the time.'

MUS: Personally, I'm not much of a talker in front of a camera. Face-to-face I'll happily chat away, I'm good at that from all my days promoting clubs, but stick a lens in front of me and I'm not so relaxed. Luckily, Ashley did most of the speaking, and Jamaal and Myles seemed pretty cool with it, too. I kind of like to hang back a little bit.

ASH: We had conversations about what it meant, why they were paying so much attention to us and whether we were going to be one of that year's novelty acts. I thought, *Either they think this is going to go horribly wrong and we are going to be a laughing stock or actually they think we could be decent*, but we really just didn't know.

Luckily, we were all pretty relaxed, we had a laugh all day. A lot of people were really tense and seemed quite apprehensive, but we literally just messed around from minute one.

JAM: There were certain points where our energy would dip and then we would have to try and perk ourselves back up again. As mates, that was easy; we were used to being around each other all the time.

MYLES: Just to complicate matters, we hadn't got clearance on a part of one of the songs we were rapping over, so that meant I had to quickly produce an alternative version that we could use on TV. So, among all this filming, I was trying to find a quiet corner to work on the music, to reproduce elements of this instrumental . . . that was stress!

'Throughout this whole time we were finding different rooms to practise in, empty spaces to keep working on our performance. Practise, practise, practise.'

MUS: One minute there was nothing to do, then suddenly the next minute they were like, 'Come on, quick! We need you guys to film this, we need to film that.' I thought we were just going there to perform – at dance comps you either get stuck in and perform almost straight away or at least there would be something to watch – but it wasn't like that at all. Throughout this whole time we were finding different rooms to practise in, empty spaces to keep working on our performance. Practise, practise, practise.

JAM: Then finally, about nine p.m., we had a call from one of the producers: 'The judges are ready to see you now.'

ASH: We were knackered by this point but still really relaxed, we were cool about it. We were prepared, we were well-rehearsed, we had thought through every tiny aspect of our performance, plus we had four judges who were sitting there waiting to hear us. The day before we had been performing at Westfield in front of shoppers who were just walking past, not paying us any attention, so in theory I thought this audition would be quite easy by comparison.

MUS: There wasn't any doubt about what we were going into the room to do. On the way through, we met Dermot and had a chat with him. He was so friendly and reassured us about what was waiting for us in the next room. He is such a friendly person – there is a warm aura about him that I really like. I took a liking to him straight away and throughout the show that vibe grew more and more.

JAM: I admit at that point it dawned on me what we were doing; the joking around stopped as we were about to sing in front of the *X Factor* judges. There was no turning back.

MYLES: You walk around this corner and then suddenly you are confronted by these four people that you have seen on TV all your life; these incredibly famous faces and absolute legends in the game are just a few metres away from you. That was weird. They were just sitting there, straight-faced, not really giving much away. I walked in first, followed by Jamaal, then Mus . . .

MUS: I tripped up on a little platform as I walked in!

ASH: Ha ha! Yes, I saw that! Cue more laughing . . .

MYLES: I remember being surprised how quiet it was. There was a ton of people over in one corner, the camera team, producers and all that, but it was so quiet.

JAM: We lined up, and because Ash was the designated spokesman of the group, he started replying to their questions. They asked our names and a little background info, but pretty soon it was time to perform.

ASH: I was just delighted to see Nicole! Earlier in the day we had heard that she wasn't going to be there so I was chuffed when she was.

MYLES: That's because you fancy her! You had been talking about her the whole day and you were so upset when we thought she wasn't going to be there. To be fair, it broke the ice a little when we joked with her about Ash's crush and she was funny, she took it all in good spirits.

JAM: Concentrate, boys. Anyway, first up was Timberlake's 'Señorita', and, well, what can I say . . . it went really bad!

MYLES: I think Simon put his hand up after only about 20 seconds and said, 'Sorry, guys, it's just not working for me.' I was crushed. I thought, *We've worked so hard for this and now we are going to be made to look like absolute idiots on TV.* Simon said he wasn't feeling it, that it wasn't working, and then he asked if we had any other songs.

JAM: We just weren't prepared for that reaction – we thought it was going to be a straight 'yes' or 'no', not, 'Can I hear a different song? What else have you got?' So that put us a little bit off guard.

ASH: We were completely shell-shocked. We had no experience of this – obviously when you are out gigging, nobody ever stops you in the middle of a song and asks you to sing something else. That kind of hit us for six. I just thought, *Oh my gosh, it's not just that this is embarrassing, this is going to be an embarrassment that everyone we know gets to see.* They had got so much footage of us by this point, where we had been ourselves – quite loud! – so I'm like, *This is going to make great TV for everyone else but it's going to be SO embarrassing for us.*

MUS: I'm not going to lie, I didn't think there was a problem with the song. It was all going as we had practised but then the infamous Simon hand popped up. At that moment all the bad things that I thought might happen if we did *The X Factor* came rushing into my head.

Then one of the producers at the side just had a word with us and said, 'Chill out, guys, you can do this, we know you can,' which was really helpful. We decided to offer them our own song, 'I'm Feeling You', instead.

I'M FEELING YOU

SO WHAT WE GONNA DO?

I'M FEELING YOU

SO WHAT WE GONNA DO TONIGHT?

I'M FEELING YOU

SO WHAT WE GONNA DO, YEAH?

I'M FEELING YOU

SO WHAT WE GONNA DO TONIGHT?

ASH: They didn't show this but then Louis said to us, 'I need you to perform this like there is a room full of people here and it really matters to you!'

MUS: I said to myself, *All these negative thoughts, they are just not going to win. Let's just have fun, let's put our all into this – this is a chance for our song to be played on TV!*

MYLES: We all gathered every ounce of our energy; we knew this was literally our last chance. I thought, *If we are going to do this, let's dig in and put it all out there* – and that's exactly what we did. By the end of the first verse the judges were clearly enjoying our performance . . .

JAM: If I look over to the boys and see that they are enjoying themselves, it tends to spark this vibe in all of us where we start to enjoy the performance more. We are four friends who really know each other, so it looks more natural and doesn't feel forced. Thankfully the judges picked up on that.

MUS: Throughout the song you could see Simon bopping his head, Louis singing along, Nicole, too, and Sharon had a big smile on her face. By the final part of the song I could sense the judges watching me, thinking, *What does this guy do?* When the part came where I dance, I just went for it – I don't even remember what I did – and Nicole shouted, 'Here he is!' and she threw her pen down and I was like, *Okay, cool, this is good, she likes us.*

ASH: I'm actually really proud of us because somehow, out of nowhere, we got a second wind of energy and just magnified things tenfold – and despite everything that had gone on we managed to perform our song really, really well. We were freestyling over the lyrics and really vibing off each other. I'm super-proud of that performance because that was the biggest moment of our lives, right there.

JAM: When we got four yeses, it was a big relief, a great feeling, especially after such a long day and the hiccup with Simon stopping us singing. And to hear later that the other auditionees outside were up and dancing was really cool.

ASH: We also got some excellent feedback along the way. Nicole said it would be nice if the rest of us sang a little bit because it would give Jamaal the opportunity to go elsewhere with his voice and we could deliver some harmonies. She also said there was 'a lot of heart' in our performance. Simon talked about how it was unusual to hear original songs on the show and that we were 'quirky' . . . it was just all good.

MUS: Simon was clearly open-minded to us doing what we wanted to do and afterwards, off-camera, he said, 'I want you guys to educate me.' That was amazing to hear – he was pointing out that the show was not used to original material being presented, that the genres we were coming from were also not the usual *X Factor* styles, so he was fascinated and excited to see what we could bring to his competition. That was a risk for him. We are an unconventional boy band/man band, but he knew there was something there.

ASH: At first we didn't really know what he meant by 'educate me', but he was already looking at the bigger picture. Only later on in the process did that statement start to make sense to us.

MYLES: And we gave Louis one of our hats . . .

ASH: And I gave Nicole one of my hugs . . .

'At first we didn't really know what he meant by "educate me", but he was already looking at the bigger picture. Only later on in the process did that statement start to make sense to us.'

MYLES: Yes, so it was worth queuing all day! Seriously though, that was a great reaction, we were so excited afterwards. We got a photo with Dermot wearing his Rak-Su hat, then we had to do even more filming, so it was way past midnight when we climbed back in the car for the long journey home. Then it was bang! Back down to earth . . . we all had work in the morning! I drove us all the way back to Watford – that was a late and very long, tiring journey. Jamaal was the only one that was like, 'I'm going to stay awake with you!' The others boys just fell asleep, ha ha! Thanks a lot!

> '**However, the harsh reality was that nothing life-changing had happened as yet: we turned up to a show, we performed, they said you have four yeses and that was it. Back to work.**'

ASH: Myles, bless him, I don't know how he managed to drive home without falling asleep because he'd barely slept the night before either! On the drive home we were all shattered but really happy — we'd gone from being very wary of auditioning for the show at all to being quite intrigued by the potential and now . . . well, now we just felt we really wanted to do well. And let's not forget, we'd just performed one of our songs in front of the judges, which was our original target. We didn't know yet if they would even air our audition, but at least we knew that we had done ourselves proud.

JAM: Apparently a load of people quit their jobs when they got four yeses but we were all still working. Just because you get through the first audition doesn't mean anything is going to change overnight — if at all. It is not necessarily going to alter your life, so we just felt it was best to keep working and stay grounded.

The next day was a blurry dream. We got home about four a.m. and were all up for work within a couple of hours. And, of course, nothing in our lives had actually changed. Yes, we'd got four yeses from the judges, but remember, no one knew we were auditioning at this point; we hadn't told anyone because we were worried it could all go wrong. Plus the show is filmed in advance, so it was really quite surreal, being back at work the next morning, just a few hours after Nicole and Louis were singing along to our lyrics and Simon was saying all those amazing comments. However, the harsh reality was that nothing life-changing had happened as yet: we turned up to a show, we performed, they said you have four yeses and that was it. Back to work.

MUS: I hadn't told my parents where I was going, I had just said I was performing up north. When we got back and I told Mum about going through to Boot Camp, she was obviously surprised but really excited for me. I'm not sure she fully understood, at that point, because although she occasionally watched the show, she wasn't a massive *X Factor* fan. Even so, she figured getting through was a good thing for us.

ASH: While we were back in the 'real world' waiting for Boot Camp, we just cracked on with business as usual. During that time we put out a video of a song called 'Crush On You', we carried on gigging, continued rehearsing. We did a photo shoot, some more acoustic shows; we just kept it moving really, still working, still gigging, still making more music.

JAM: We prepped a whole load of music, wrote lots more new material, it was full-on. We didn't know what the set-up for Boot Camp was going to be, so there was this element of being a little bit in the dark, but we worked around that by keeping massively active. Practically, it was quite hard to plan time off work and where we would be staying during Boot Camp, all that, but they were just details that needed to be sorted. The point was, we were through.

> '**We didn't know what the set-up for Boot Camp was going to be, so there was this element of being a little bit in the dark, but we worked around that by keeping massively active.**'

MUS: We knew that for Boot Camp you can't really prepare anything because you have to choose the song at the time, so instead what we did was practise a tune of ours called 'Knock Knock' for the arena audition, which was the next stage if we got through.

JAM: We spent loads of time not only rehearsing but trying to get songs cleared. That was probably one of the hardest parts about being on the show. Legally you have to get the producers of a song to agree to it being used on TV. If we couldn't get a song cleared, then Myles would have to spend the rest of the day refixing a beat.

'At Boot Camp
we were like, Cool,
here's a whole load
of new people,
new experiences.
Let's have some
fun with this and
see where it goes.'

MYLES: That's when it started getting intense: writing, rehearsing, clearing songs, coming up with choreo, little dancing parts for Mus, beatboxing opportunities. We met up at Ash's house every day and went through every tiny detail, rehearsing there for hours and hours.

Going to Boot Camp, I was taking unpaid leave, so that made it feel more serious, too. It was costing us money, so we had to look at it professionally and approach it correctly. That's partly why we rehearsed and prepped so much, but mainly because that's just how we have always worked.

ASH: When the time came to head off to Boot Camp, again we weren't really very tense or emotional. Our view was, we'd got through Round One and performed 'I'm Feeling You', which would hopefully be broadcast later on the show, so in a sense it was already job done. That took away an enormous amount of pressure. At Boot Camp we were like, Cool, here's a whole load of new people, new experiences. Let's have some fun with this and see where it goes.

MYLES: On the first day of Boot Camp, we ended up sitting outside for a few hours while they waited to film everybody arriving. We met all these new people, faces I didn't know, and I wondered how far they were going to go in the competition. I really felt weird at first: here we were at the Boot Camp of a show we'd all watched for so many years and now we were inside this TV bubble. It was just like, *Waoh! Are we really doing this?*

MUS: I think we were pretty focused during Boot Camp. Our view was, this isn't like a summer camp where the priority is to have fun. Without wanting to sound ruthless, we were not there to make friends or anything like that. I'm not saying that we didn't, we made a lot of friends, but that wasn't the priority. The aim was to work hard, prepare and then deliver our performances to the best of our ability.

I remember meeting loads of groups and asking, 'How long have you guys known each other?' and they'd say a few months, or sometimes a few weeks! Some had even been put together for the show and had only met a few days' earlier. That made me think that what we had was special, because we are friends first before anything else.

MYLES: In between rehearsals, I felt we were still getting dragged around more than most people, which I hoped was a good sign. We legit weren't nervous and in fact a few times the camera crew were like, 'Are you guys really that relaxed?' I think they were used to people being more unsure, but that's just how we are; we are four friends having a great time, so why would we be nervous?

ASH: The first day was the Wall Challenge and we were given instructions to pick just one song. Song choice can mean everything, the difference between success or rejection. If we'd ended up with a power ballad, for example, we'd have been completely screwed and no doubt gone home. So, we all picked either really high or really low cards from specific points on the wall, then we huddled together to decide which was the best song we had collected. Bruno Mars's '24K Magic' was the best option so we quickly put the other cards back!

MUS: I thought, *Okay, cool, this is an uptempo, vibey song – we will be able to have fun with this.*

JAM: There were five acts in our line which proved to be a little bit . . . not necessarily difficult, but we just had to make sure that we picked a certain part of the song that we could put our own stamp on, where Mus could beatbox, the boys could rap and I could sing.

ASH: Jam is right, we had to be pretty firm and focused on that. We didn't really get involved in too much discussion with the other acts about how the song was going to be broken up. Everyone else was trying to learn the words to the song, but pretty quickly we were locked into figuring out how we'd change the song to fit us.

MYLES: We dissected the song, started writing to it, chopped out this part for me, Ashley was figuring out how to rap while Mus was working on where he would beatbox. Another day of staying up till three a.m. rehearsing. There's never an early night on *The X Factor*!

MUS: Fortunately our group worked together really well. There was no rivalry or inconsiderate behaviour, it was a good line of singers. We all knew that we had the same goal. We practised together, as well as on our own, so we were lucky to have nice people alongside us.

ASH: That day was so long. Unfortunately, in the actual performance I forgot my words, even though I wrote that rap myself! Myles bailed me out and I ended up freestyling – I'm pretty sure what I said didn't make that much sense, but at least it wasn't too obvious at first glance that I had messed up, especially with Myles covering me.

MYLES: It really wasn't that bad, Ash, and besides, I was happy to help! After we'd all finished, the judges didn't actually comment too much on it, which was a little nerve-wracking.

ASH: I came off and I was honestly gutted. I felt so, so bad because if we'd been sent home it would've been my fault. Personally I was not in a good place, but luckily we managed to get through and the boys supported me like true friends do.

'We all knew that we had the same goal. We practised together, as well as on our own, so we were lucky to have nice people alongside us.'

MUS: When we were invited to step forward and some singers weren't, I was like, *Okay, this is getting a little bit real now; these people are going home right now, it's all over for them.*

JAM: That was the first time that it hit home how brutal the process can be – it was heartbreaking when the other acts from our line went home. When we were working out the song, we'd started to develop a little bit of a bond and a relationship with a few people, so to see them sent packing was tough. It was a pretty blunt reminder that this was a competition.

MYLES: We actually got quite close with some of the acts. For example, Boot Camp was the first time I met Sean and Conor Price. They were sat in a circle with an Irish girl group and Sean was playing his guitar, they were all singing together. I heard this and I was like, *I'm going to go over there and rap!* I literally went over, pulled up a chair, sat down and started rapping along with them. That was great fun, everyone was buzzing and they all had smiles on their faces. After I stopped rapping, I picked up my chair, moved it to one side and walked off again. It was only the other day that Sean told me how, after I had left, they were all amazed and said how cool they thought my rapping was, which was a really nice thing for him to say!

JAM: After that we had the arena auditions, which was the first time we had ever performed to so many people – I think it was maybe 4,000, which was crazy!

ASH: If *X Factor* hadn't have happened, we were planning on releasing an EP, so we had some songs stacked up. As Mus said earlier, we'd already been rehearsing one particular tune for this stage, 'Knock Knock'.

MYLES: We started rehearsing with the show's vocal coach, Annie. We had never worked with a vocal coach before, so that was a real eye-opener. She had us doing a three-part harmony for the first time ever, and she was so good at explaining and helping us.

'We never kept things back for a later stage, if that makes sense. We just ran with our best material straight away. Let's face it, if you hold back, then get booted out, you will always wonder what might've been.'

ASH: We knew the song, we were comfortable with that, so it was a case of learning how to harmonize with each other, which, to be perfectly honest with you, was an alien concept. We were like, *Okay, we have never done harmonizing before, so why don't we do it for the first time in front of 4,000 people?!* We thought 'Knock Knock' was our best song – we never kept things back for a later stage, if that makes sense. We just ran with our best material straight away. Let's face it, if you hold back, then get booted out, you will always wonder what might've been.

MUS: Watching it back now, I think the harmonizing sounds really bad, but at the time we thought, *Oh, it sounds sick! Oh my gosh, that's it, we are like Boyz II Men now!* Joking aside, though, I think that was the start of us actually working on our vocals and how we were all going to sound together, helping each other out in terms of singing.

ASH: We came up with a little bit of choreography, nothing too special, just a couple of steps here and there. When our names got called to perform, we went out there and . . . *Wow!*, what a reaction we got from the crowd! It was the biggest crowd we had ever played to *by a country mile*. However, everything was made so much easier because as soon as we stepped out on to the stage, everyone just started cheering and screaming. That instantly settled our nerves because it was like, *Okay, the audience is with us already, they are willing us to do well and be good.*

JAM: The atmosphere was electric, it was just an experience like no other because we had never performed in front of a crowd of that size. They went wild!

MUS: Instantly I was like, *Okay, this is going to be fun!* You just get so much energy from those screams. When Myles said, 'Hello, Wembley!' the noise was incredible! How can you not feed off that?

JAM: I actually feel that wasn't our best performance; however, it was exciting, it was a new experience and one that was made even better by the crowd engaging with it and us having fun onstage. I guess, if you had asked us four or five months earlier about the idea of performing at Wembley Arena, that would have been incredible, so to have that experience and be received so well was just amazing.

ASH: That was the first 'Myles moment'. He kind of stepped out in front of us to rap and the audience's reaction to him was just insane, the roof nearly blew off! All the girls were basically going crazy. After that we got into the song and people just seemed to really, really enjoy it.

ASH: Somebody asked me the other day if that moment, hearing the screams at Wembley, was the first time we thought we could win *The X Factor*. I have to be totally honest here and say that winning the show was *never* even a thought for us… well, not until the night before the final. Winning *The X Factor* became a concept twenty-four hours before we did it. Up until that point, it was just about getting through – so for example, the arena audition was another chance to perform a song of ours to 4,000 people; if we got booted out after that, we could release that song and the whole experience would've been a progression. We genuinely just wanted more people to hear our music. That generated much less pressure, as we said earlier, because for us it was more about living in the moment and just getting through each stage, one at a time. We never looked past what we were doing each day, we never had one eye on the next stage. It was always about how we were going to deal with what was confronting us in that moment.

MUS: After 'Knock Knock', Simon asked us what the song was about and Jamaal explained that it was about a girl next door that he liked, so he went round to speak to her. Simon said, 'What happened after you went round and knocked?' and, I don't know why, but I piped up with, 'She didn't open!' Everyone burst out laughing and that seemed to me to be a good sign – they were enjoying us having a laugh and being relaxed onstage.

Then it was decision time and the crowd was screaming for us to be put through, so when the judges gave us another four yeses the place erupted! We were so, so pleased!

ASH: Performing in front of 4,000 people for the first time was obviously a massive occasion for us and it meant lot. Directly after, when we came off stage, Myles got really emotional. My aunt, who worked for my mum's business alongside Myles, had sadly passed away not too long before that and I remember Myles got really emotional thinking about her, which in turn led to me getting emotional, too. We felt like she was looking down on us through the whole thing and we wished she could've been there in person. That arena audition was a little bit unfathomable, so to be thinking of my aunt in that way with the boys was a stand-out moment during the process, for me personally, anyway.

MUS: One last story to tell around the arena auditions: after they had finished, we were taking pictures outside the venue with loads of people and there was a bunch of kids there in a dance group. They were really excited and said, 'Do you want to see one of our routines?' They did this routine outside of Wembley Arena for us and Ash said to me, 'That's because they like what you do, they want to impress you. You are influencing them, Mus.' That really hit me, I guess you could say I was pretty overwhelmed.

MUS: Next up was the Six Chair Challenge. Savage! At this point we didn't know who our mentor was going to be, so they put us into a room with all the groups to find out. In my head I thought, *All the judges have been around for such a long time, they will all help us out in their own way.* I probably preferred Simon or Louis: Simon just because he knows everything there is to know about the music industry, and with Louis, I felt because we are so different, that he would have passion and fight for us. Don't get me wrong, Nicole or Sharon would've been amazing, too; let's face it, they're all so experienced.

As soon as we all saw Simon's head pop round the door, everyone else started screaming and running towards him. However, in complete contrast, we got in a huddle on our own and said, 'Right, we've got Simon. We need to think fast: what do we ask him? Let's come up with questions – we need to make the most of this opportunity.' So, there was no celebration, just immediate focus again.

JAM: The producers came over and said, 'Hey, Rak-Su, is everything okay?' because it was just a completely different reaction to the other contestants in the room. We explained we were great and I think they understood that we were just taking a moment to make the most of this new development. I guess it almost looked as if we weren't happy – we were, but we were also very focused, if that makes sense.

We realized how much hard work this process was going to be and made sure that every time we were in somebody's presence who could potentially give us information we maximized that opportunity. Not just the judges but the whole back-room team – they are all very experienced in TV, live shows, music, so you would be mad not to learn everything you can from all of them.

In the lead-up to the Six Chair Challenge, we came forward with a whole batch of songs such as 'Mamacita', 'Palm Tress', 'Change Your Mind'. . . all this new material. 'Palm Trees' quickly got vetoed, then they crossed off quite a few of our songs fairly rapidly. However, after some discussion about covers and other song ideas, we eventually settled on 'Change Your Mind'.

'In the lead-up to the Six Chair Challenge, we came forward with a whole batch of songs such as 'Mamacita', 'Palm Tress', 'Change Your Mind' . . . all this new material.'

'By this point we were starting to panic. We eventually got called to the stage but only when all the chairs were already taken, so to win a place in the next round we would have to uproot someone else.'

MUS: We had never actually performed that song to an audience before; we'd sung it in front of the production team in rehearsals but never in front of a proper crowd. And this audience just happened to be several thousand people at Wembley.

JAM: Some of our family were there so we were all excited but also keen to make them proud. It really helped because that night is really savage.

ASH: Personally, I've always liked Six Chair Challenge. Watching it on TV, I thought it was funny and made for great entertainment. I actually really enjoyed being a participant, too, although it is definitely less comfortable than watching it sat at home!

At first we were watching all the other groups do their thing, and some of them were getting love from the crowd but mostly everyone was getting booed; it was ferocious at times. By this point we were starting to panic. We eventually got called to the stage but only when all the chairs were already taken, so to win a place in the next round we would have to uproot someone else.

MYLES: We went onstage, started the song and immediately it was a rave up there! We had no choreo, it was literally just a jolly-up onstage – we had a mad one. I was shouting down the microphone, I lost all composure, I literally sprinted down the end. Ashley was way over there, Jamaal and Mus were going mad in the middle, just raving. We gave it our all, onstage in front of thousands of people at Wembley. I was literally screaming and the boys bantered the life out of me over that later. It was so funny.

ASH: I went up one aisle, the boys spun off in all directions, the whole arena started dancing and we just literally had the time of our lives. We were shouting, it was pitchy, we looked a mess, but we just went crazy! It was sick!

JAM: I think that performance was probably one of the most euphoric moments in the whole *X Factor* competition, because we went out, the crowd got right behind us and we had a blast. They were chanting, 'Rak-Su! Rak-Su!' It almost felt like it was our own concert.

MYLES: I remember seeing all these thousands of people smiling and everybody jumping as we neared the end of the song. Nicole was going crazy – it was mad, I think she put her leg up on the table at one point! When the song stopped, people just carried on screaming, so we knew it had gone down well. Almost immediately the crowd was shouting, 'Put them through, put them through, put them through!'

MUS: Louis told Simon there was going to be a riot if he didn't put us through!

JAM: Eventually Simon chose to replace Beau Road with us for Chair Two. That was great news for Rak-Su but we were also sad for those girls, because we had got to know them and they were really lovely people. So it was a bittersweet moment, to be honest, but of course we were grateful.

MYLES: We were buzzing but we didn't really show that, out of respect to the girls in Beau Road. We didn't want to jump up and down so we just walked over there and hugged the girls, didn't make a scene.

JAM: However, we weren't through yet because there were other acts to follow who could steal our chair. That is not a nice feeling, waiting, especially when there were so many great performers coming after us. You go from the absolute high of being given a chair to quickly realizing that it means *nothing*, that you might still be going home. Sitting there waiting to see if we were going to be kicked off, I think the boys were a little bit more confident than I was. All the artists after us were absolutely on point, they were so good, so I did have my concerns. However, one by one they performed and yet we were never replaced. I remember thinking, *Wow, I cannot believe that we are still sat here!*

ASH: Honestly? I thought it was fun! It was a bit like being on a rollercoaster. It was nervy because somebody would come out and do something really good, but it's a competition, and I think all the sports that we did throughout our lives equipped us well for that evening. Every time Simon started pondering what to do, I sat there thinking to myself, *Don't say Two, don't say Two!*

MYLES: After every performance I looked over to Louis, Nicole and Sharon and they were talking amongst themselves, pointing at which acts they thought should go and I was trying to figure out their signals and read their minds. It was pretty mad but I just had a feeling we would make it through.

JAM: At this point I thought it would be amazing to get to Judges' Houses, but I also thought if it didn't happen, then at least we had sung at Wembley, we had performed to this huge crowd, had that amazing feeling. Sure, it would be great to replicate that again but if that didn't happen, then at least people knew us, they now had a good idea about our songs and that would help us moving forward.

ASH: The waiting just got worse because right at the end Simon decided to have a three-way sing-off. I thought that if he told us to do an *a cappella* performance against these other really amazing vocal groups we were going home. However, that never happened, we didn't get booted off . . . and that's when it sunk in – we were going through to Judges' Houses! I don't think the audience ever shouted for us to lose our seat, so we have got the crowd to thank for making it through the Six Chair Challenge.

> Somehow we had got through to Judges' Houses . . . the Promised Land.

JUDGES' HOUSES

'After the Six Chair Challenge, we all went back to work again. Reality bites once more! It was harder this time, because my mind was somewhere else.'

I was working on the reception of a hotel, checking people in, dealing with flight delays and all this hassle, but my mind was on Judges' Houses with Simon Cowell. That was a surreal feeling!

MYLES: It was at this point in the story that the TV show caught up with itself, by which I mean they finally broadcast the first auditions, including ours in Manchester. Up until this point only close family knew what had been happening, so getting time off work had been tricky for some of us, and keeping quiet about the whole *X Factor* experience was a challenge!

ASH: On the Thursday before the Saturday launch show, Sharon was on a breakfast TV show talking about *The X Factor* and they showed a clip of us from the auditions – we didn't know about this and we were all at work. Suddenly people started coming up to me, saying, 'Er, Ash, I think I just saw you on TV. Are you on *The X Factor* for real?' and I was like, 'Er, yes, actually!' In the space of a few hours our Facebook page went from 1,000 to 10,000 likes and I was like, *Okay, this is very, very weird. Something is going on here . . .*

JAM: The next day the show posted something about us on their official *X Factor* Facebook page, as well as other social media sites. I was at work when they did that – my phone was vibrating off the desk, people were calling and texting me, it was going crazy. Remember, most of our friends didn't even know we had entered the show, so when this social media stuff happened, everyone went nuts. Work became Rak-Su Central basically, and I couldn't do anything without them all knowing – they were really nice and supportive. Previously, work and singing had been two completely different areas of my life that I never mixed, but now everyone knew! Personally, it was when the show went public that I started to feel we were a part of the competition for real.

MYLES: The following night the launch show was going to be aired on TV, so we got all our friends and family around to my house. There were about seventy people in my front room, it was packed out. We had our speakers connected up to the TV so everyone could hear.

MUS: When the show started – the new season of *The X Factor* – everyone was buzzing but at the same time we weren't sure if we'd even be on. Maybe we'd be one of those acts that just gets a few seconds' screen time here and there, then eventually goes home and makes virtually no impact. We just didn't know.

MYLES: Imagine our shock when the first faces we saw on the programme were ours! We say hello and walk in . . . and then all our family and friends went completely crazy, the room exploded! I remember thinking to myself, *Wow, we've just opened Season 14 of* The X Factor, *we are the first people on it.* I knew that was a good sign.

ASH: They aired a good three minutes of our back story and then our audition of 'I'm Feeling You'. I was *amazed*. It felt like they had used us almost as the poster boys for the new series.

Immediately after that first show being broadcast was such a crazy period. People started to get in touch with us about bookings and paying us good sums of money. The most we had ever been paid before had been about £250, but suddenly people were talking about £2,000 or more per gig. Our Spotify and SoundCloud streams went through the roof, as well as Facebook likes, Twitter followers, Instagram comments . . . everything just exploded. Then a friend called me up and said, 'Ash, do you realize you guys are Number 1 on the Spotify UK viral playlist with 'I'm Feeling You'?' That song had been out on the *Dive* EP for about six months by this point but had never really done anything commercially, yet now suddenly it was Number 1 on that playlist; then we found out it was Number 38 on the iTunes download chart and even in the official UK downloads chart at Number 82! *Everything* had changed overnight. This was insane.

MYLES: Yes, it just went completely nuts, like Ash says. Also, in our general day-to-day lives around Watford there was a lot more attention and excitement once that first show had aired, but at the same time we knew there was still work to be done.

ASH: Absolutely. After the Six Chair Challenge, you've got about six weeks to go away and get ready for Judges' Houses. I think in that time we wrote about twenty new songs in preparation for the next stage, and we were rehearsing constantly, every single tiny aspect of each performance and song. I ended up buying three different books on songwriting just to understand and study the craft even more. The boys all read them, too. We started to really delve into the art. Jam started to take vocal lessons so his voice went from strength to strength, and Mus started to really experiment with his dance; Myles started to get more into production – we were all super-focused. Essentially, we were attempting to upgrade ourselves for Judges' Houses.

'I'd been striving for years to study a masters degree and at this point in the Rak-Su story I had just been offered a place, so this was a very serious moment for me. To turn down that opportunity, I had to be certain that Rak-Su was absolutely serious, that this was what we all wanted to do 100 per cent, and so to see the boys work so hard before Judges' Houses meant I knew declining the masters was the right decision.'

JAM: I'd been striving for years to study a masters degree and at this point in the Rak-Su story I had just been offered a place, so this was a very serious moment for me. To turn down that opportunity, I had to be certain that Rak-Su was absolutely serious, that this was what we all wanted to do 100 per cent, and so to see the boys work so hard before Judges' Houses meant I knew declining the masters was the right decision.

MUS: We were all still working at this point, so it wasn't until Judges' Houses that we finally decided to quit our jobs. That meant not having any income, so it wasn't a decision to be taken lightly. Jam had turned down that masters, Myles and Ash resigned from senior managerial positions, my hotel work had been going great, so it was a risk, but we just felt it was time to focus on the band without any distractions whatsoever.

In contrast to all those daily practicalities, it was really exciting when we found out we'd be travelling to the south of France for Simon's Judge's House! Before we flew out, we went to what they call 'routining', which is where you sort out the songs you are going to sing. They told us to come with a good selection and they were surprised when

we presented them with nine of our own original songs, no covers. We just felt we had to be pretty determined, we needed to dictate what we would perform. I would much rather get knocked out doing one of our own songs then go through by performing someone else's.

MYLES: That's exactly how we all felt, Mus. All or nothing.

ASH: Like Mus says, they were surprised, yes, but we made our point politely but firmly: 'This is where we are at; we've been writing non-stop, it's all original material.' You have to choose two songs, only one of which gets aired. Pretty quickly it was narrowed down to three: 'Palm Trees', 'Mamacita' and 'Call Me'.

MUS: It was still very much step by step, we had no thoughts of winning or the Live Shows. We just made sure that the songs we agreed on were going to be fully prepared and go down well, by working with the production team and the vocal coaches, and just really grafting to make sure everything was perfect.

ASH: You might wonder why we were all so thrilled to get to Judges' Houses, when in previous rounds we had been very much more laid-back about progressing. The simple fact was Judges' Houses would guarantee that we were on TV again in front of the entire nation. And not just a 90-second performance – there'd be in-depth interviews and coverage. We knew that this could be life-changing for us because we'd got loads of new songs in the pipeline and Judges' Houses would enable us to start releasing songs after the show. It seemed like such a massive potential springboard.

JAM: I wasn't thinking of winning yet, though, were you?

ASH: No, not even for a second. Mus?

MUS: No, same. One step at a time. Personally, I didn't even think of that. I wasn't looking too far into it, I just wanted to get this next stage done, get through and then think about what to do after that. To be fair, we knew it was getting serious now, but none of us were thinking of winning. We'd even had people telling us we were going to win but we just didn't think like that. I was aware, though, that we were starting to get a lot of attention across the UK.

MYLES: Absolutely. I remember finding a website called Digital Spy, looking up Rak-Su and seeing that people were going crazy about us, bigging us up, saying we were going to win, all that, so I knew we had a lot of support.

For example, on the day we flew out to France, we got to Gatwick Airport, and as we were walking into the entrance of the terminal, there was a security lady who just shouted out, 'I'm feeling you! You lot are sick, you guys are going to win it!' Me and the boys just started cracking up, it was so nice. We jumped on a plane, went over to Monaco and immediately went to do more filming. The Judge's House was a magnificent villa surrounded by these beautiful mountains – you could see for miles and miles.

'On the day we flew out to France, we got to Gatwick Airport, and as we were walking into the entrance of the terminal, there was a security lady who just shouted out, "I'm feeling you! You lot are sick, you guys are going to win it!" Me and the boys just started cracking up, it was so nice.'

MUS: I remember saying it's not like a villa, it's like a vill-age! When I'd initially heard we were going to Monaco, in my head it was going to be like a holiday – this was actually our first trip away together. Turns out it wasn't a holiday at all! Judges' Houses was hard work, very long hours, early mornings and late nights, a very compact three days, but fantastic at the same time.

JAM: That villa looked like something from a movie – there were random antiques and interior design items scattered around and hanging from the walls; there was even a grand piano in one room. It was all very lavish.

MYLES: On that first night away, we had a moment to ourselves during an hour's break. I remember saying, 'Let's go for a walk!' So we went to this little pebble beach nearby and I wanted to go in the water but the boys weren't so keen. Whenever one of us wants to do something that none of the others do, we have this private banter where we say, 'If I was to die tomorrow and you hadn't done this, how would you feel?!' So I laid that line on them and they had to come in the water then, no matter how cold it was! It was beautiful though, crystal clear, and you could see thousands of fish – amazing. I was soaking it all in, standing there with my best mates in this sparkling water on the Monaco coast, our band was through to Judges' Houses . . . then suddenly we looked at each other, it was a big realization: *Wow!* Just a fantastic moment where we were able to pause, take in what was happening to us and appreciate everything.

JAM: That was the first time we actually sat back and thought about where we had got to. We were away from home as brothers for the first time ever, and it was brilliant to share that experience with them. If it had all come to an end then . . .

ASH: Don't say we would've still been happy, because we wouldn't!

JAM: No, fair enough! We wouldn't have been happy, correct. But at least we would have been to the south of France and had that experience.

In terms of the other contestants, yes, there was this element of camaraderie, but at the same time it became very obvious in Monaco that there was a lot more competition in the air; people were practising much more intensely, it felt like everyone was raising their game for Judges' Houses. People were aware that the Live Shows were around the corner and getting through to that stage can be genuinely life-changing, so the effort everyone was putting in was very high. There wouldn't be 15 minutes when you didn't hear somebody rehearsing.

MYLES: Having said that, we wanted everyone to do well. We didn't see it as a competition. The Price brothers were our boys, we looked after them, we cracked banter with them all the time. That's when we formed our supergroup called Rak-Price!

ASH: True, but Jam is right, it was suddenly very clear that we were involved in a serious competition. For example, there was a girl group called Lemonade and their harmonies were just on point, they practised them religiously. Now, up to this stage I had kind of considered us to be the hardest workers in the process, something I was quite proud of, but at Judges' Houses, occasionally we would be lounging around and then I'd realize Lemonade were rehearsing . . . that was a

'The Price brothers were our boys, we looked after them, we cracked banter with them all the time. That's when we formed our supergroup called Rak-Price!'

stark reminder that we were there to work, to get down to business. It gave our work ethic the extra kick to graft harder than everyone else.

MYLES: The day before the performance, Cheryl flew in by helicopter and when she landed, I said, 'Boys, she looked at me!' They bantered me for that!

ASH: Yeah, *sure* she did, Myles, even though she had mirrored sunglasses on so we couldn't tell! To be fair to Myles, as soon as she landed in the helicopter we were egging that whole situation on, 'Myles, she's definitely looking at you!' Naughty really, but it was great fun. We did banter him pretty savagely about that. For ages after, I was singing, 'Myles is in love with Cheryl . . .' Really childish, yes, but fun all the same!

MYLES: You're still bantering me now! Anyway, changing the subject, no matter how much filming we were doing or how long the hours were, it was still a perfect day, set in this amazing villa, surrounded by mountains, hot weather and with my best mates.

JAM: The night before our performance, we sat down and chatted and I said, 'Look, we are ready, we are rehearsed, this is our own song, we know what we are here to do . . . *but we need to go through.* We have worked this hard, we have pushed this far, so let's go out there tomorrow and give this everything.'

MUS: The next day, the performances started and everyone was immediately brilliant. The Cutkelvins went out, then Sean and Connor Price, and they were all absolutely blinding. I remember seeing them perform and I was just like, 'What?!' Everyone was strong; we felt that the groups were the best category in the competition. But we couldn't see us getting through as well as the Cutkelvins, because we thought we were too similar.

'We did banter him pretty savagely about that. For ages after, I was singing, "Myles is in love with Cheryl . . ." Really childish, yes, but fun all the same!'

MYLES: We ended up being the last group to perform, so we were thinking, 'Why have they picked us last? Is this a good or bad thing?' You had to go down a little walkway and there was like a pond in the middle near where Simon and Cheryl were sitting, then you just stood in front of them. It was late at night, dark, time to perform. I know some people find performing in front of two people intimidating, but to be fair we weren't nervous.

ASH: As we were walking towards them, we were laughing and joking – it was very rare during any part of the process that you would catch us being anxious or serious. Simon and Cheryl were warm and welcoming, so that made life easier, too.

MUS: When we walked up to them, I heard Simon say to Cheryl, 'Watch out for this guy, he will surprise you!' Anyway, we did 'Palm Trees' and the performance felt fun, vibey, it was cool.

MYLES: They seemed to be loving it. Cheryl's face was beaming; she was smiling, rocking in her chair, bopping to the song and Simon was smiling, too, his face was lit up. It seemed like a great reaction but, of course, they don't give much away.

MUS: At the end I started beatboxing and I remember Cheryl going, 'Oooh, okay!'

ASH: We did ourselves proud with our performance and I felt we'd done all we could. When we finished, Simon clapped and said, 'You've done well, guys, you really have!' Then he said, 'You have the ability to write hit records . . .' and we were like, 'Waoh!'

Cheryl said that when we were rapping it sounded 'so London' and that was important for us, too. I loved that comment because throughout the whole process we had been scared that someone was going to try to turn us into something we weren't, but now we were being congratulated for just being ourselves.

JAM: Cheryl also said we had a global appeal and that we could do well in America. Coming from her, that compliment was a really big deal.

ASH: Every comment was complimentary. The only question mark was from Cheryl about the choreography . . .

'Cheryl said that when we were rapping it sounded "so London" and that was important for us, too. I loved that comment because throughout the whole process we had been scared that someone was going to try to turn us into something we weren't, but now we were being congratulated for just being ourselves.'

> 'Later, Simon said, "When did you guys write this song?" and we explained it was a few months earlier and he said, "This is a hit song. I really like it. That song is big, especially with the current genre of music playing now. I really love it."'

MUS: She told us to think about choreography more because if we were to go through to the Lives, then that part of our performance would become significantly more vital and all I could think of to say was, 'Soon come!'

Later, Simon said, 'When did you guys write this song?' and we explained it was a few months earlier and he said, 'This is a hit song. I really like it. That song is big, especially with the current genre of music playing now. I really love it.'

ASH: We always take constructive criticism on board. Back when Nicole said we needed to harmonize, we went away, studied that and started to learn how to do it. So when Cheryl talked about choreo, it was the same: okay, go away, learn, study, make it happen. We have always been of the view that if we don't know about something we will find out about it.

JAM: Anyway, when it comes to decision time at Judges' Houses, it's pretty intense. All six groups sit in a room waiting, then one by one they are called down to go and see Simon. It's a five-minute walk and we were the last ones left in the room.

MYLES: You are totally isolated from the other acts. You haven't heard any results before you go out; you have no idea who is through and who is going home. It's pretty crazy.

MUS: When the third act left the room, I thought, *Those three could have been sent through and we could be the ones that are sent home and that's it, all over.* It was incredibly nerve-wracking.

MYLES: While we were waiting, we told ourselves we loved each other and then, as we walked to meet Simon and hear his decision, out of nowhere we started singing Chance the Rapper's 'Blessings'. It is just a beautiful song, it felt like such a positive moment.

Simon was sitting in this stone seating area with his shades on. The camera crew were all there and we had built up a great relationship with them – we would never kick up a fuss about anything behind the scenes so they liked us and would constantly banter us and shout, 'Rak-What?!' all the time. However, when we got to Simon, they didn't look at us or give us any indication of his decision – they couldn't spoil the reveal, obviously.

ASH: My gut feeling was that our performance had gone well, but I still didn't know which way it was going to go. We had performed exactly how we wanted, so I had no apprehension about being shown on TV. If we'd gone home right then, well, at least we had showcased ourselves in the best light possible.

MUS: I remember standing in front of Simon, cameras everywhere. He was wearing his sunglasses, the sun was out, this magnificent vill-age was behind us, we were waiting to find out if we were through to the Lives . . . it was an intense moment.

MYLES: Waiting for his decision was literally just pure silence. Worse still, you can't see his eyes because of his shades. Then finally Simon started telling us about his decision-making process, but as he did so, a plane flew over and the camera crew said, 'Stop!'

JAM: Obviously the plane noise disrupted the audio so we had to start all over again. Incredibly, that happened another two times. Simon started, only to be interrupted by more plane noise – stop again, restart, it was agonizing! We had to keep reshooting the reveal, and of course we didn't know yet what his decision was, so it was incredibly tense! When the planes eventually stopped, waiting for Simon to finally give us his decision was just the longest 45 seconds of our lives!

'While we were waiting, we told ourselves we loved each other and then, as we walked to meet Simon and hear his decision, out of nowhere we started singing Chance the Rapper's 'Blessings'. It is just a beautiful song, it felt like such a positive moment.'

MUS: Finally he said, *'I'm gonna be seeing you in the Live Shows!'* Oh, wow! Did I just hear that correctly?

JAM: That was incredible! Such a moment of pure elation!

MYLES: When he said we were through to the Lives, I seized Mus and Ash's chests, literally grabbed their T-shirts, while Jamaal jumped up and shouted, 'Yes!' What a moment!

ASH: In those moments, more than anything I tend not to notice how I react but how the other guys feel – I felt Myles's hand push against my chest, I could see the pure elation in their faces. Jam was jumping in the air, Mus was speechless. It was brilliant!

MYLES: The camera crew were clapping and cheering us, then Simon said, 'If I had sent you guys home, the crew would've killed me!'

MUS: It was just a massive relief. I thought, *I don't know if this is real, but it feels real; can it be true?* What an incredible moment in my life. Simon gave us all a hug and let me tell you, he gives really hard hugs! He slapped me on the back and I think I've still got a red mark now!

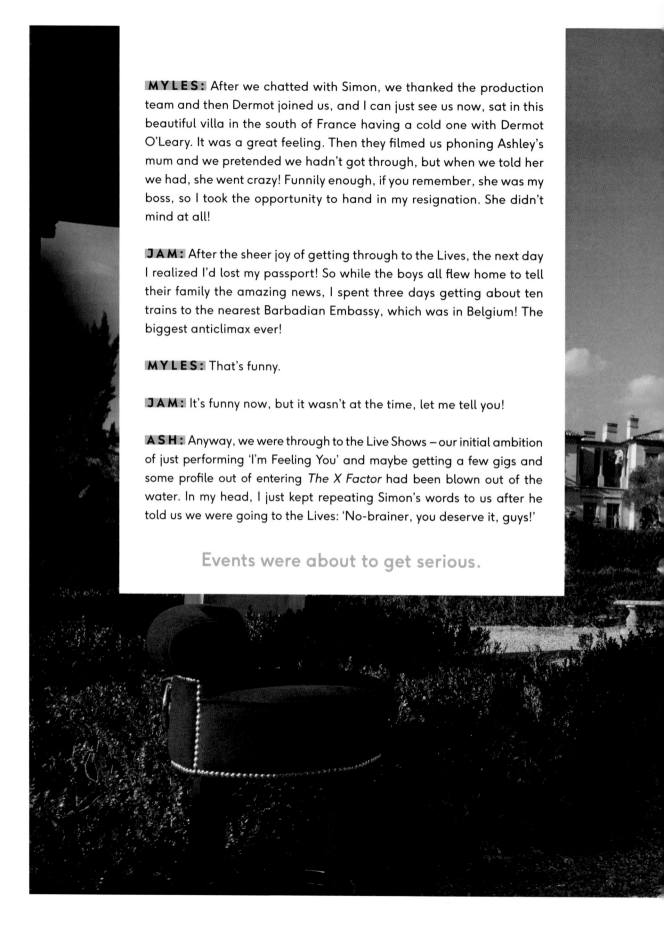

MYLES: After we chatted with Simon, we thanked the production team and then Dermot joined us, and I can just see us now, sat in this beautiful villa in the south of France having a cold one with Dermot O'Leary. It was a great feeling. Then they filmed us phoning Ashley's mum and we pretended we hadn't got through, but when we told her we had, she went crazy! Funnily enough, if you remember, she was my boss, so I took the opportunity to hand in my resignation. She didn't mind at all!

JAM: After the sheer joy of getting through to the Lives, the next day I realized I'd lost my passport! So while the boys all flew home to tell their family the amazing news, I spent three days getting about ten trains to the nearest Barbadian Embassy, which was in Belgium! The biggest anticlimax ever!

MYLES: That's funny.

JAM: It's funny now, but it wasn't at the time, let me tell you!

ASH: Anyway, we were through to the Live Shows – our initial ambition of just performing 'I'm Feeling You' and maybe getting a few gigs and some profile out of entering *The X Factor* had been blown out of the water. In my head, I just kept repeating Simon's words to us after he told us we were going to the Lives: 'No-brainer, you deserve it, guys!'

Events were about to get serious.

THE LIVE SHOWS

'Ahead of the Live Shows, a lot of people were telling us this was the big step up, but we still didn't want to get carried away – we viewed this as just another bonus round, basically. The only real challenge at the start of the Lives was adapting to living in the *X Factor* house with all the other contestants; all fun and games really.'

MUS: Moving in was weird! The house was amazing. I have never lived in a house that big, or with so many people. It was so luxurious but at the same time it felt like student accommodation. Having to share a room with the rest of Rak-Su on bunk beds was slightly odd, twenty-five-year-olds bunking up in one room, but it was fun!

JAM: Yeah, right, for about a day, ha ha!

MUS: You're defo not wrong!

MYLES: The house had a swimming pool, gym, a games room, everything that you could want. I love cooking, so to me the stove was amazing, I was buzzing about that! It was great to meet up with all the other acts, and the atmosphere in there was always good. I don't think there were any arguments to speak of, everyone got on pretty well.

JAM: Myles is right, the *X Factor* house was pretty swanky. Having said that, it became less and less swanky as the weeks went on, because we were all working 15-, 16-hour days so no one had any energy to tidy up much!

On the first day in there, the production team explained to everyone about the general rules of being in the *X Factor* house, like not tweeting, because the show hadn't caught up with itself as yet. We were still living inside this TV bubble.

Personally, I noticed there was just this whole air of greater focus; all the contestants were ready to come out fighting and smash it, so we knew that we had to up our work rate yet again, no excuses.

MUS: Rak-Su kind of had our own little eco-system in the house and didn't really get too involved in what everyone else was doing. We felt we had a job at hand, to work hard and make the most of every moment.

ASH: The first week of the *X Factor* Live Shows is interviews, interviews, interviews! Sometimes we'd be doing three hours' worth of set-up, prep, filming and reshooting, but then the final clip would only last about two minutes.

We also had wardrobe for the first time, which was a stress because we suddenly had other people dressing us and they didn't necessarily get who we are, our fashion sense and what we wanted to wear. That was a battle at times. I didn't have my first outfit confirmed until the morning of the Week 1 show, because I just didn't like what they were trying to put me in. I felt like a proper diva!

'Personally, I noticed there was just this whole air of greater focus; all the contestants were ready to come out fighting and smash it, so we knew that we had to up our work rate yet again, no excuses.'

'One of the vocal coaches. He talked us up, telling us we needed to believe in ourselves more. Remember, I'd never sung or rapped before, so I didn't know where my range was or anything like that. I never said I was a singer, I never said I was a rapper, I'd always come as a dancer and a beatboxer, but during *The X Factor* I learnt how to be part of a music group.'

JAM: The lead up to Week 1 was fairly easy, in my opinion. The theme was 'Express Yourself' and Simon wanted us to perform 'Mamacita', which really helped because we knew that inside out, so the pressure was off. Really all we had to do was rehearse a little bit of choreo, sort the outfits and get accustomed to the TV staging. There was a little bit more pageantry now, and obviously because it was going out live on national TV you had to make sure that everything was on point. Even so, I think that Week 1 was probably the easiest week we had during the Live Shows.

MUS: When they said Simon really liked 'Mamacita', that felt like a vindication of sorts, it felt like testament to our gut feeling that our songs could work. I was so energized that week, I just felt, *No matter what, we have to fight for it even more now.*

We worked hard with the staging and choreographer that first week. Obviously I knew how to dance onstage but that was always for a live crowd; now I had to learn staging for a camera. Suddenly it wasn't just about the movements I was doing, it was *where* I was doing them. It was fascinating.

One of the vocal coaches, a guy called Lil' Eddie, really helped us that week (as did the other coach, Annie). He talked us up, telling us we needed to believe in ourselves more. Remember, I'd never sung or rapped before, so I didn't know where my range was or anything like that. I never said I was a singer, I never said I was a rapper, I'd always come as a dancer and a beatboxer, but during *The X Factor* I learnt how to be part of a music group.

ASH: For the first weekend of the Lives, we were quite fortunate to go on last on the Sunday, so we got to see everyone else perform, we heard the crowd, we saw the atmosphere, how the broadcast team worked – that was really helpful to relax our minds. Another key moment was when Dermot called out the names of everyone who was performing – our

scream was slightly louder than everyone else's. Only ever so slightly but it *definitely* was, so we all looked around at each other and were like, 'Waoh, people might like us here guys!'

On the night, the performance of 'Mamacita' went absolutely flawlessly and the audience seemed to love it, the judges gave us amazing feedback and we won the vote and flew into the second week. What a way to start the Lives! We were just absolutely buzzing! Better still, our song ended up peaking at Number 3 on the iTunes chart as well!

MUS: My parents came to Week 1, which was a big moment for me – it was a really good feeling seeing my dad in a Rak-Su hat and T-shirt! All our families were incredibly supportive throughout the whole process. When I heard about 'Mamacita' doing so well on iTunes, I just thought, *This is nuts, we are Number 3 on the iTunes chart!* We never thought that would happen . . .

JAM: Everyone is faced with a challenge on the *X Factor* Live Shows, but perhaps we took on more than most, because we were determined to perform original material *every week* – that meant writing new songs constantly throughout the process, week in, week out. The least we wrote was six songs in a week, the most was nine. We just felt very creative and inspired and, to be honest, the pressure just seemed to ramp that feeling up even more. Nonetheless, choosing to perform your own material is a big risk. The reality is that you don't know how well the public are going to react. They have never heard these songs before – they might hate them. We kept taking that risk week after week.

Behind the scenes, constantly writing new songs for each show created an immense amount of work. To be fair, the show's production team were very accommodating. There was an issue of trust: would our material be good enough to broadcast every Saturday to millions of people? Would it be too much new material too soon? Would we remember the new lyrics each week? How would the public react to the new songs? Occasionally we had to be persistent when they suggested that we did covers instead, but I think the public helped us massively, too, because anytime we performed our own material it seemed to get a better reception. This was not an approach that *The X Factor* was famous for, so the team had to really make room for that and we are very grateful that they did. We were going to either die by our own sword or fly by our sword.

'In my opinion, Week 2 changed everything: the audience absolutely loved 'Dimelo', we won the night, got to Number 1 on iTunes – we were just in a daze, to be honest. Creatively, this endorsed our decision to perform original material.'

MYLES: Totally agree, Jam. Plus I feel it pushed us on, too, because we were doing so well with these songs; we had to come back every week with better and better material to just keep that progression going. We couldn't rest on our laurels.

MUS: For Week 2 – Latin Week – Simon initially wanted us to do a mash-up of 'Wild Thoughts' by DJ Khaled featuring Rihanna and Carlos Santana's 'Maria, Maria', but we were like, 'Er, not really sure about that!' So we went away for an hour and worked on a song called 'Hold Up', which we really liked. We even changed some of the lyrics into Spanish and felt it worked great, but when we rehearsed it in front of Simon, he wasn't convinced; he said there was something missing. That's how 'Dimelo' came about. We have written songs at the most peculiar times, under the biggest pressure, but sometimes that makes you more creative. Fortunately, when we performed 'Dimelo' that night we got the most amazing reaction!

MYLES: At the end of each show, waiting for your name to be called to get through to the next week was just mad. At first it was nerve-wracking, but as the weeks went on we relaxed more and would just be bantering about it. When you are standing onstage waiting, they play this sound like a heartbeat – duh duhn. Eventually we started doing this little dance in time to the beat, so while everyone else was looking stressed, we'd be doing this little dance step and laughing. It all helped us stay relaxed, I guess.

ASH: In my opinion, Week 2 changed everything: the audience absolutely loved 'Dimelo', we won the night, got to Number 1 on iTunes – we were just in a daze, to be honest. Creatively, this endorsed our decision to perform original material.

MUS: Totally agree with you, Ash. After being told to do the mash-up of the covers and saying no – politely but firmly – the subsequent success of 'Dimelo' proved that we had a sense of what could work.

ASH: We were just on cloud nine at this point. Then came Week 3 . . . which hit us like a bombshell. The original theme was 'Crazy In Love', so we wrote 'Mona Lisa' with that in mind, but for very obvious reasons the theme got switched to George Michael Week. Now, George Michael was a legendary artist and we all thought of him as the icon that he is rightly regarded as, but in terms of music, we were a bit lost for what we were going to perform . . . the fit wasn't obvious.

JAM: We were asked to sing 'Faith', a massive legendary song. We'd prepped 'Mona Lisa' but that was out of the window now, so this was quite stressful. Simon sat down with us and said, 'Look, guys, you know I think your originals are great but I just think that this will be a good way not only to pay homage to a great artist but also to give people a break from originals.' When he said that, we were all thinking, *A break from originals? But that's what we do. Is he fed up with our material?*

MYLES: We were confused and trying to second-guess him. *Does Simon want us to go home? Is he trying to get rid of us?*

ASH: I kind of had a bit of a strop with myself about it. I wasn't entirely comfortable. I was writing my verses with a frown on my face at first. I was just in panic mode because I felt we were not prepared for this. After speaking to fellow contestant Grace Davies and the boys, I thought, *Do you know what? It is what it is. Let's honour a great artist and make this work.*

MUS: Being totally honest, George Michael wasn't an artist I was particularly familiar with, but I am delighted we had that week because it really helped me understand music and open my mind to other styles. I watched a documentary on him, which taught me what an incredible artist he was and what he went through, so after seeing that, the amount of respect I had for him was crazy. As tricky as that week was, it was definitely an educational experience for me.

ASH: We were on first that night, which is always hard because the audience is a little bit cold. We performed 'Faith' and it was just okay. I remember coming off and thinking, *That was not good.* In comparison to 'Mamacita' and 'Dimelo', that was our worst performance so far, by a long way. Totally out of our comfort zone. I thought there was a strong possibility we would be going home, to be completely honest with you. Beforehand we'd been told that it was a double-elimination week as well, so I was convinced we were goners.

JAM: I agree to a certain extent that 'Faith' threw us off balance a little bit and we had to figure out how we were going to get over that hurdle; we were very uncomfortable. However, we took on the challenge and tried to make it our own, while still being as respectful as possible to the great man himself. In retrospect, singing the George Michael cover was a fantastic opportunity for us to grow as an act; it was a big challenge and I'd like to think we rose to it. It just forced us to be more dynamic and adaptable.

MUS: Like Ash says, we did the performance and we were all like, 'Okay, that's it, we're going home.' As much as that would've been annoying, our original aim of having 'I'm Feeling You' played on TV had been achieved.

ASH: Yes, but at that point, standing onstage waiting for the results of Week 3, I was absolutely cacking myself, especially when we were left until the bottom two. Stressing out!

MYLES: We all know that acts are put through 'in no particular order', so being in the 'bottom two' does not necessarily reflect the votes you have won. However, when you are stood onstage waiting, it doesn't feel like that; you just feel gutted. Luckily, we managed to wriggle our way through, but that was the most stressful and taxing week of the Live Shows.

'In retrospect, singing the George Michael cover was a fantastic opportunity for us to grow as an act; it was a big challenge and I'd like to think we rose to it. It just forced us to be more dynamic and adaptable.'

MUS: Looking through social media and reading the newspapers, some people liked our version of 'Faith' but some people absolutely hated it. We were accused of being disrespectful to George Michael by changing his song, but we just tried our best to do what we do, whilst paying a respectful tribute and homage to him.

MYLES: I was proud of that week, too. We were doing a tribute to one of the greatest artists who's ever walked this earth – with rapping, and it just felt like we were asking a lot of the audience to buy into that. We thought we had screwed up, but actually it got a huge response as well as the most online views that week and even a chart place, too.

ASH: On a lighter note, George Michael Week also gave birth to the first time we ever said 'Pyro-ting', just a silly private Rak-Su joke that became a little bit of a catchphrase for us. When we went to rehearsals that week, it was the first time we'd ever had pyrotechnics and it was really hot and Jam was like, 'Arrggh! Pyro-ting!' Then he started singing, 'Pyro-ting,' then Myles joined in and then me and Mustafa, just messing about, being silly. After that, for every rehearsal and performance we'd sing 'Pyro-ting' to each other. It was just a little ritual to help us relax.

JAM: After Week 3, the show started to become a routine and we were kind of on autopilot. In the house we were just working all the time: if it wasn't writing, it was rehearsing, or talking through choreo, just all these little details; I remember feeling quite early on that we seemed to rehearse more than everybody else.

'On the night, 'Mona Lisa' went down really well, which was great because we got to bounce back to what we wanted to do. We won the night, and that song then went to Number 1 on the iTunes charts, so that was a big relief, to be back on track.'

MUS: We were also having vocal coaching and choreography, it was pretty full on. Remember, we were novices to the whole TV production game. We were just totally consumed with preparation and practice.

ASH: For Week 4, oh gosh, we were originally going to perform our song 'Mona Lisa' with female dancers in a kind of a sexual way. Some people said it was a good idea, some people said it was bad, so we were in two minds about it. We weren't entirely comfortable, so we went home and stayed up until about two a.m., figuring out alternative choreography for the performance. Bear in mind we knew nothing about choreography! We all sat around a laptop watching loads of videos of other groups and dancers, just so we could kind of understand more. The next morning the decision was taken to cancel the female dancers, so it was lucky that we'd already worked out a new routine.

On the night, 'Mona Lisa' went down really well, which was great because we got to bounce back to what we wanted to do. We won the night, and that song then went to Number 1 on the iTunes charts, so that was a big relief, to be back on track.

JAM: Looking back, I really enjoyed that week and we even ended up winning the prize fight on that night, scooping the chance to go overseas and work with the great songwriter Ali Tamposi. At the same time, for me personally there was never a week where I thought, *We absolutely smashed that, we are definitely not going home.* I still went from week to week, one step at a time.

MUS: By now I was having a lot of fun. All the hard work, all of the performances, I was enjoying everything. If I recall correctly, at one point we had five songs in the top ten on iTunes!

At the same time, you have no real indication of how events are being received in the outside world, you are very much in an *X Factor* bubble. We didn't know how many people actually knew who we were, we didn't know how many people were voting for us – in many ways we were completely in the dark. Then one of my friends who works in a school told me that the kids he taught were all talking about Rak-Su and they didn't believe that he knew me – that's when I realized something was going on.

JAM: By the semi-finals it had started to get quite quiet in the house. We went from everyone being in this massive, busy house to there being only a few acts rattling around in there.

MUS: The semi-final was held over two days, split into 'Cool Britannia' and 'Songs to Get to the Final'. For the first night, when you think of typical *X Factor* songs, you might consider maybe Elton John or the Beatles. However, because of the type of people that we are and what inspired us as kids, we thought of garage. The idea of showcasing garage on *The X Factor* really appealed to all four of us – that was a very exciting thought.

ASH: Handling a double performance was a little bit stressful, but again, it was cool: it is what it is. That week we were all given 'in-ears', which are bespoke fitted earpieces that enable you to hear the correct sound balance onstage. That was a treat, it made us feel like real artists – it's funny what sticks in your mind, isn't it?

First up for us in the semi-final week was a garage song by Sweet Female Attitude called 'Flowers' – having grown up listening to garage, it felt great to be paying homage to that.

'By now I was having a lot of fun. All the hard work, all of the performances, I was enjoying everything. If I recall correctly, at one point we had five songs in the top ten on iTunes!'

MUS: Rehearsing that song brought back a lot of memories of going to Destiny's under-18s nights in Watford, all the parties that we used to go to as friends, just great times — and now here we were, preparing to sing it on a massive live talent show in front of millions of viewers. It was such a buzz.

However, at the Friday rehearsal, Simon could sense we weren't entirely happy. I said, 'I'm personally not comfortable with the choreographed dancing. I feel like there should just be a huge, mad party onstage, because that's how I feel when I listen to this song.' To his immense credit, Simon went with that and said, 'Okay, fair enough, then we are going to get rid of the choreo. Let's do it your way. I'll get it sorted.' What a vote of confidence that was!

On the night, 'Flowers' worked brilliantly. We had all these people partying onstage with us, it was great. In the clip you just see me going nuts, I was having a rave!

'The second evening was 'Songs to Get You to the Final' and we chose 'I'm Feeling You', which was a really emotional moment for us, coming full circle from our first audition.'

ASH: The second evening was 'Songs to Get You to the Final' and we chose 'I'm Feeling You', which was a really emotional moment for us, coming full circle from our first audition.

MYLES: The problem was, some of the production team didn't want us to do 'I'm Feeling You', not because they didn't like the song but because they felt it was a risk doing something that we had already performed.

MUS: However, we stood our ground and insisted. That song had got us there in the first place, and we wanted to be able to do it again but beefed up on this big stage, step it up even more. Yeah, like Ash says, that was probably the most emotional performance that we did, not just the song itself but everything that it represented.

MYLES: Thankfully, on the night, people lost their heads when we performed 'I'm Feeling You' again! By that point everyone watching knew who we were and seemed to love us. We had the chart success behind us, plus the response we were getting from the general public was ridiculous, it was just surreal. I felt it seemed to peak with 'I'm Feeling You' and for me personally that was a hugely emotional performance. I broke down in tears after. That was the first song we wrote together as Rak-Su, and it just meant so much to us. It was a very powerful moment.

ASH: The performance was really well-received and gave that song a chance to shine – the next day it went to Number 1 on the iTunes chart. That was a fantastic moment. Remember when we had sat down eight weeks after the abandoned food festival gig in Shoreditch and talked about entering *The X Factor*? About how we wanted to perform 'I'm Feeling You' on TV *once* . . . well, now we had done it *twice* . . . and we were in the *X Factor* semi-finals. Amazing.

Even so, despite what you might think, we were still not thinking about winning the competition. Personally, I was like, 'Okay, this is going well, let's keep working.' Logically I couldn't see that we were going to win at the time and also to a degree I didn't want to believe in that idea too much, because I was a little bit scared of setting my sights too high, in case we failed.

JAM: As it turned out, Ash, we didn't fail. We didn't get knocked out. The public did like what we were doing. On semi-finals results night we were voted through and into the final.

We had made the top three of *The X Factor.* How crazy was that?

THE FINAL ... & BEYOND

'During the week leading up to the *X Factor* final, there was only us, Grace Davies and Kevin Davy White left in the house, so on the one hand it felt very quiet, but the atmosphere was still pretty intense and it was all about the competition.'

They then moved us to a hotel nearer to the arena. By now every act was exhausted; we were all coming down with a virus or feeling under the weather. It was cold outside, snowing in fact, we were probably getting four or five hours' sleep a night and were pushing ourselves as hard as we possibly could every waking hour of the day.

ASH: I don't think we went to bed before three a.m. all week and we were up early every morning, preparing. We were just trying to cover everything from every angle. For example, on the Friday night before the final, we were all up until about three thirty a.m. getting our hair done, because we just hadn't had any time during the day for a haircut! We meticulously worried about the smallest details and rehearsed the tiniest elements over and over again.

JAM: We took our 'Battle Bus' back to Watford, to our old school; we even ended up playing football at Watford FC! The support we received from our local town was just unbelievable. I will never forget that.

MYLES: With only three acts left, the production team had fewer people to worry about, so it was really chilled backstage. Even so, we still wanted to go out there and smash it. We made the decision to have fun that week, onstage, backstage, before, during and after. We wanted to enjoy it, savour the final week of *The X Factor*.

On the day of the final, we actually walked to the venue; it was freezing but we strolled over there, had some breakfast and got down to rehearsals. We were even drinking camomile tea, that's how chilled we felt!

ASH: Mind you, camomile tea or not, at first we were stressed because there is always a group number to perform at the start of the show. This week it was 'You've Got the Love' but for some reason we didn't get told until two days beforehand, so we didn't start rehearsing until the day before. This was not a song that we would normally do, so that was an uncomfortable start to the final weekend.

On a positive note, just before 'You've Got the Love' began at the start of the show, they called out everyone's names to the crowd. Now, progressively through the Live Shows, the screams for us had been getting louder and louder in comparison to everyone else. That night the screams for us in comparison to the other two – I really don't want this to sound over-confident – there was a *substantial* difference. That helped us relax and the performance itself went okay; we did it with slightly gritted teeth but got through it.

JAM: When the time came for us to perform our first slot, we sang 'Mamacita' and the crowd went crazy! The reaction and noise was like nothing we had ever heard before, the whole arena was screaming, 'Rak-Su! Rak-Su! Rak-Su!' That's when it started to sink in a little bit more. I thought, *People are loving us, they are loving our music, something must be going on.* It felt like another level of support and *that* was when I started to wonder . . . *Maybe, just maybe . . . we might win this!*

MYLES: It was just mad, people were out of their seats, stomping on the floor and screaming. The place erupted. It was scary how loud the response was compared to the others.

ASH: I just couldn't believe there were that many people showing that sort of emotion for us. I actually almost turned around, I thought they'd maybe sprung a surprise star onstage behind us; maybe Justin Bieber had walked on at the back or something like that. *People can't be screaming like this for us – it's got to be some sort of mistake.* For me, *that* was the first time where I kind of looked to my left and right at the boys and thought, *Waoh, we might actually win this thing.*

MUS: I couldn't have described it any better, Ash. Seeing the crowd cheering for us, banging their feet, waving, chanting, just the sheer amount of energy and noise that they had for us, was nuts.

'Myles always dreamt a little more than the rest of us. He would actually get quite annoyed at me because I'd be saying stuff like, "It doesn't matter if we win it or not, as long as we do ourselves justice and portray ourselves in the right light," but Myles would be like, "You're annoying me, stop saying stuff like that. We are going to win."'

ASH: Myles always dreamt a little more than the rest of us. He would actually get quite annoyed at me because I'd be saying stuff like, 'It doesn't matter if we win it or not, as long as we do ourselves justice and portray ourselves in the right light,' but Myles would be like, 'You're annoying me, stop saying stuff like that. We are going to win.' That's how Myles thought about it.

MYLES: Mmm, I dunno, beforehand I think deep down I still wasn't convinced we were going to win it, though. It didn't seem right because there has never been a group like us on *The X Factor* before, who write and perform their own originals so much, with two rappers and a beatboxer/ dancer, too. Little Mix were the only group that had ever won it previously. I also felt that Grace was a ridiculously good singer, Kevin was amazing as well, so I couldn't really see it happening for us . . . but after 'Mamacita' sent the venue into meltdown, something inside told me that we might just have a chance . . .

MUS: Our second song that night was 'Dimelo'. It's such a fun song, any time we perform that, anyone who is sitting down instantly just stands up and dances. The amount of videos that we get sent of someone's kid dancing to the song, or even parents and grandparents dancing . . . it's such a good vibe! However, this time we would be performing with two absolute icons of the music industry, Naughty Boy and Wyclef Jean!

JAM: That was a crazy experience! Naughty Boy came into the dressing room beforehand and he was just bouncing off the walls, he was so energetic, one of those people that lifts the energy in the room as soon as they walk through the door. He said he really digged our song.

MUS: Naughty Boy's from Watford as well — he actually went to the same school as me, Myles and Jamaal, Westfield. We met him way back before the very first audition came out on TV and he spoke to us about the music scene and educated us a little bit about it all, so we had his support from the very beginning. To then be onstage with him . . . that was a good thing, man, that's putting Watford on the map right there!

JAM: Then shortly after, another talented soul, Wyclef Jean, walked in the room! Surreal! We were sitting there, chilling with these two amazing artists, then Wyclef started playing 'Sweetest Girl' on the piano in the corner of the room. Amazing memories.

ASH: Wyclef was a really interesting character— he is full of so much youth and energy and is a very cool guy. He was really eager to help us out and lend a hand and onstage he is such a great performer.

MYLES: Absolutely, Wyclef is such a big personality. We just jammed out and he was playing the keys and singing. For me that was weird, seeing such a legend and talking to him about life. Same with Naughty Boy, we were just chilling and cracking banter.

MUS: I used to listen to a lot of Fugees, old-school hip-hop, so that was a big moment for me. Wyclef was telling me how during the Fugees days he used to do breaking, so there was a little connection there, and he said I reminded him of a guy called Crazy Legs, who is an old-school B-Boy (break-dancer) — the same dancer who hosted the B-Boy Championships at Brixton Academy that I went to way back in 2006. Amazing.

'Then shortly after, another talented soul, Wyclef Jean, walked in the room! Surreal! We were sitting there, chilling with these two amazing artists, then Wyclef started playing 'Sweetest Girl' on the piano in the corner of the room. Amazing memories.'

'We started performing 'Dimelo' and immediately everyone was up out of their seats, there was fire (pyro-ting!), it was just mad onstage and then Wyclef comes on crawling along the floor like a worm, so weird and yet so fantastic. Naughty Boy is there on the beat pad and it was literally a party onstage.'

———————

MYLES: Then we got to do the performance with Wyclef and Naughty Boy . . . not before we did our little 'pyro-ting', obviously! Even in front of thousands of people, before the *X Factor* final we have to do the pyro-ting!

ASH: Wyclef mentioned in rehearsals that he might come out and slide on the floor, but we didn't think he would actually do it! The only problem was that when he was sliding, his in-ear came out, but like a true pro he recovered and the whole crowd absolutely loved it.

MYLES: We started performing 'Dimelo' and immediately everyone was up out of their seats, there was fire (pyro-ting!), it was just mad onstage and then Wyclef comes on crawling along the floor like a worm, so weird and yet so fantastic. Naughty Boy is there on the beat pad and it was literally a party onstage. The noise was just ridiculous. People were going ape.

MUS: That was just a whole bag of fun onstage; it was literally just a party. Wyclef coming on the way he did was just nuts, then him going into a handstand at the end of the performance – he is an absolute legend.

JAM: That was hype, that was a good performance and the crowd went crazy for that. We had fun onstage and basically left it all out there, then hoped for the best. It felt like this was where we wanted to be, this was what we wanted to do for the rest of our lives.

The first night went brilliantly well and we knew that whatever happened we had already boosted our profile more than we could have ever imagined. As for winning . . . well, several big acts had come second or lower in the final – Olly Murs came second and One Direction came third, and they both seem to have done okay! However, I'm not going to pretend otherwise: by now we wanted to win, we really did.

MUS: Kevin went home first, which was a sad moment. He is probably the nicest guy you could ever meet; if he had gone through instead of us, then I would not have cared at all.

MYLES: We were appreciative of the fact that we were on a live TV show in front of millions of people, so we didn't get over-confident – we still had that final hurdle to get over on the Sunday. We never took anything for granted; there was always too much work to be done.

ASH: When they'd called us through to the final day, I thought, *Okay, let's go and win this now. We have come this far, let's go and take it home.* Simon called us up to his dressing room and we knew he hadn't won the competition for a while. He said, 'Guys, you've done really well, but I don't want this to be it. I don't want you guys coming second, to just be another talented act that comes second or third. Now you are here, go and win it.' Such inspirational words.

JAM: We left the arena really early in the morning but when we got outside there were some fans waiting in the snow . . .

MUS: I thought, *This is surreal! Are all these fans waiting for us?!* But they weren't! They said, 'Have you seen Louis?'

I thought, *That's amazing, they're waiting in the snow for Louis Walsh,* so I said, 'Yeah, I've seen Louis,' and they were so excited.

'Oh, we love him, we love Louis!'

I was a bit taken aback and then it dawned on me. They were waiting for Louis Tomlinson from One Direction, who had been rehearshing ahead of his performance the next night!

ASH: We made the decision not to rehearse when we got home because we were absolutely knackered. We decided we would actually be better off getting some sleep.

JAM: The Sunday night of the final was actually very business-like. Sam Smith, Pink, Little Mix and CNCO performed and it felt as if it was a concert that we were booked to play with loads of other acts.

We saw some of the other contestants floating around backstage, which was really nice, but we were still trying to keep our focus. Even when the arena was full of people and various guest performers were onstage, we weren't watching them, we were rehearsing.

Backstage, the boys kept saying four words to me all day: 'Today's a good day.' I was thinking to myself, *What the heck are these guys talking about?* but I didn't pay too much attention to it. Then I suddenly thought, *Oh my gosh, have they brought my dad over from Barbados?* Then lo and behold, we suddenly had a mystery 'interview' – and who walks up the stairs: my father! What an amazing thing for them all to do! I was so touched and obviously really pleased to see him. Mind you, we didn't have much time to chat as there was more singing to be done!

ASH: The first song we did that night was 'Touché', a new song that nobody knew, but Dermot overheard us rehearsing it in the dressing room and said that it might be his new favourite song of ours! However, during the performance itself, we got to the first verse and Myles forgot some of his lyrics . . .

MYLES: Thanks for reminding me, Ash! We rehearsed that song over and over again, we read the lyrics, we rapped the lyrics time and again, we were *seriously* prepared. Then, like Ash says, for some reason when we walked out there I forgot my words! I started the first verse well, but then just before the second four bars . . . I blanked out. So I had to freestyle and I guess that's where all those years listening to grime and freestyling with Ash and my friends came in. I was able to think on my feet and make it work. I think it actually turned out all right but, even so, I was fuming with myself.

ASH: To make matters worse, I then messed up the choreo! The whole performance felt a little bit haphazard. Me and Myles were completely gutted with ourselves. Jam and Mus were really supportive and throwing positivity at us, but I was like, 'That really wasn't good. I'm so sorry, guys.' Then a member of the production team came over to us and said, 'Guys, Simon wants to speak with you really quickly. Meet him at the back of the stage *now*!' This was in an advert break so we ran over, met Simon and he said, 'Look, guys, I really didn't like the choreography on that, it really wasn't great, but you know what? That is all behind you now, just let it go, it's history. You've got one more performance to go out there and win this thing. Just make sure with the next song that you pull it out of the bag. Go for it!' That was exactly what we needed to hear, to be honest, because we agreed with him. 'Touché' wasn't great but now we had a chance to put that right.

JAM: The last song we performed on *The X Factor* was 'Mona Lisa'. I thought that if we were going to come second I wanted to do so with my head held high and no regrets. Obviously we knew that song inside out, so thankfully it went really well, it went to plan and we did ourselves justice. Finally . . . we were done. Now all we had to do was wait for the results.

MUS: It's probably only about fifteen minutes or so before they announce the result. You go backstage and basically just wait. Then we were escorted on to the stage and stood next to Simon. Before the result was announced, I had my eyes closed and I was praying. I don't know what I was praying for, I was just thankful for where we were, regardless of what happened next.

MYLES: I was kissing a bracelet on my wrist that I wear to remind me of Ash's late Aunty Nicky. I always used to say a prayer before every result and think of her.

JAM: Then Dermot said the famous words: 'The winner of *The X Factor* 2017 is . . .'

ASH: Dermot read out the result really quickly, but in my head it took *forever*. I could have sworn the gap between Dermot tee-ing up the announcement and then saying our name was *hours*! When he shouted, 'Rak-Su!', ah, I just lost control basically. I jumped on top of Mustafa, got him in a headlock, Jamaal hugged Simon, Myles just ran off, Simon was giving people the most ferocious hugs and slaps on the back . . .

MUS: I heard our name called out and I opened my eyes like, What! Ashley jumped on top of me, I had my head in my hands in disbelief, Ashley's mouth was wide open, screaming in my ear!

MYLES: I ran off to the front of the stage . . . I don't know what the rest of the boys did, I couldn't tell. I fell to my knees and I was just like, This is mad!

ASH: It was just the most amazing feeling. Euphoric. We'd done it!

MUS: The feeling of pure elation was overwhelming, amazing. I can't remember exactly what happened next, I just felt so good. I still haven't watched the episode back yet, just because the feeling that I have now, telling this story, I want to keep that. I reckon if I was to watch it back and see how we all react, I would probably cringe, and I don't want that to happen.

MYLES: We had done it. We were the first ever male group to win *The X Factor*. And the first winning act to perform original songs, too. Plus we were now going to release the first single to be written by the winning act.

JAM: One of the best moments of that whole night was when we were performing the winner's song with all the other *X Factor* contestants. That was ridiculous. I remember giving a mic to Sean Price and he ended up singing loads of the lyrics!

MUS: It just didn't feel like it was real at all. I remember thinking, *We don't have to worry about going through to next week, we don't have to worry about anything. It's all done.* After the result, everything was just quick, quick, quick. Like Jam says, we did the winner's song and had a massive party onstage with all of our friends. There was confetti and fire everywhere, everyone was just having a massive party. That was a really good feeling.

ASH: Louis was dancing, Sharon was dancing, Simon was dancing, Dermot was dancing — it was just amazing. Nicole was up, too, so I kind of grabbed her hand and danced with her onstage. A cool moment for me, personally! When you listen back to the performance, we are all shouting: it's not singing, it's not rapping, it's just shouting! But it didn't matter because the whole arena was partying with us.

'It just didn't feel like it was real, at all. I just remember thinking, *We don't have to worry about going through to next week, we don't have to worry about anything. It's all done.*'

Everyone had cried at some point during the process for one reason or another, whether it was thinking of a loved one such as Aunty Nicky, whether it was when we heard supportive messages recorded by our families, whatever, all the boys had cried, but I hadn't. After the show stopped being broadcast and we were all left up onstage, I saw Jamaal, so I went over to him and gave him a hug and I just started crying then . . . it was just too much for me . . . I remembered where me and Jam had started and what the boys had just done. It was so far away from where we began . . . we had won *The X Factor!*

MUS: Eventually we got back to our dressing room, got changed, gathered all our stuff and then they took us to Simon's dressing room, where we met all sorts of record industry people, and Wyclef and Naughty Boy were there, too. The amount of hands I shook!

JAM: The rest of that night was a massive celebration and all about the party; it was an amazing feeling, an incredible conclusion to our journey. We eventually made it to the Just Eat after-party, and as we walked in they said, 'And here are your *X Factor* winners!' All our families were there waiting for us and there was a huge cheer – what a feeling! Simon introduced us to some of the performers from the night and then said a few words to everyone. I think it was only then that it sunk in that we had actually won the show.

MUS: Simon made a toast to us and said, 'Thank you for changing the show . . .' which I am assuming was because of the original material we performed each week. That was a weird feeling. I almost stepped back from myself and thought, *That's Simon Cowell, and he just toasted us as* X Factor *winners!*

We all hugged our families for ages. I hugged my dad longer than I have ever hugged him, then I hugged my mum for at least five minutes solid. Throughout the show our mothers were all known as Mum-Su, so by now people knew who my mum was – that was weird!

JAM: We left the venue well after midnight, but we had to be up at dawn to drive to a TV studio around six to be on *Lorraine*. Crazy, it was absolutely crazy.

MUS: I don't think I even slept at all, maybe half an hour's kip?

ASH: Me neither. In the days after the final, everyone got ill, immediately! All of the adrenaline was gone, all the tension had evaporated; the weeks of living in that house, not exercising properly, not always eating properly, being cooped up and not getting fresh air, it all just hit us at once and everyone's energy sources were drained.

JAM: I was so tired. We were running on fumes. Lorraine was lovely the next morning but I have to be honest, after that the rest of the week went by in a blur, basically. Radio, more TV, interviews, photo shoots – it was non-stop, super-exciting and super-exhausting! Brilliant fun.

MUS: In Winner's Week I honestly couldn't tell you what we did. The amount of different radio stations that we went to, from Kiss to Capital, speaking to loads of different DJs and journalists, going to different places, filming all the time, it was all compacted into one week of mayhem!

MYLES: Mind you, we stayed at a lovely place, the Royal Garden Hotel, for a few days – that was sick. I had £50-worth of room service every night for free. I would order everything on the menu, nachos with pizza with burgers with spaghetti bolognese with crisps with chips . . . I never ate it all; I was just having it large and living like a king!

MUS: We've done some amazing events since winning the show. The National Television Awards was an incredible night. Seeing Sir David Attenborough so close was very surreal, and there were people there from *EastEnders*, *Coronation Street*, Ant and Dec, Phillip Schofield, Holly Willoughby, all these famous people that I'd seen on TV.

'I was so tired. We were running on fumes. Lorraine was lovely the next morning but I have to be honest, after that the rest of the week went by in a blur, basically. Radio, more TV, interviews, photo shoots –

it was non-stop, super-exciting and super-exhausting! Brilliant fun.'

ASH: The Jingle Bell Ball was another really cool moment. When they announced the list of names, I swear we got a louder cheer than everyone else and I was thinking, *Hold on a second, Sam Smith and Dua Lipa are on this line-up. How come people actually even put us in the same category?*

MUS: That was our biggest performance, in front of 20,000 at the O2. Nuts. We sang 'I'm Feeling You' and 'Dimelo'. I remember thinking, *This isn't to try to get through to next week; this is just us, performing onstage in front of all these people, this is how it is going to be.* That was a wonderful feeling.

We also did a performance for Grenfell — that meant a lot, and being around the aftermath of that awful tragedy brought us back down to earth and made us realize how completely blessed we are.

JAM: We pretty much crawled to the finish line of that week's media commitments. Our last performance was at G.A.Y. at about one thirty on the Sunday morning. My gosh, honestly, I remember getting back home that morning and literally falling straight to sleep. I don't think I woke up till maybe one p.m. the next day!

'Then we got ready for the *X Factor* tour, which was a great experience, made even better by the fact that we hadn't gigged for a little while, plus we were on the road with all our friends from the show, so it was great to catch up with them all.'

The very next week we had an immediate opportunity to get in the studio to experiment and write some songs, and that has set the template for what we have been doing since winning the show. Our original material is what won us the competition, and that is what we need to create more of moving forward.

In February, we went to The Brits which was amazing, seeing all these super-famous artists. Then we got ready for the *X Factor* tour, which was a great experience, made even better by the fact that we hadn't gigged for a little while, plus we were on the road with all our friends from the show, so it was great to catch up with them all.

ASH: Since winning *The X Factor*, we have been writing and writing and writing, just trying to develop as artists, because we realize we need to be constantly thinking about how we can improve. We are going to take dance and singing lessons to work on our choreography and harmonizing. Improvement was the one constant throughout the whole *X Factor* journey for Rak-Su, and that cannot be allowed to stall.

'I knew that whatever I focused on I was going to do to the best of my abilities, but I've been lucky that I found three other people to embark on that journey with me.'

The first three months of 2018 were kind of just about figuring out our new world, finding the balance in our new life and trying to develop and learn in a lot of different areas. We already work much harder at this than we ever did in our previous jobs, but why wouldn't we? This is our opportunity to solidify the dream.

MUS: Just because we won the show, that doesn't mean that we are going to take a break and relax. We still have a lot of work to do – in fact we feel like the work is only just starting.

JAM: I feel the ambition is to get a Number 1 single. Then release a global record, a piece of material that we can stand behind and say, 'Here we are, we are Rak-Su, we are proud of this music.' *The X Factor* is a huge show in the UK but overseas some countries don't even air it, so we have a lot of work to do to bring Rak-Su to those audiences. We need to write a song and an album that can transcend those international borders, then back that up with hard work, touring and yet more songs.

ASH: I've been blessed to be able to spend so much time with three people who are positive and like-minded and that will always be a positive influence on me. My mum and her siblings have all done really well for themselves, coming from a village in Cameroon where going to school and electricity were a luxury, so growing up for me was always a case of, If they have managed to do well and be successful from their hard beginnings, then with the head start that I've had, I've got no excuses. I knew that whatever I focused on I was going to do to the best of my abilities, but I've been lucky that I found three other people to embark on that journey with me.

JAM: Someone asked me the other day what I would say to the kid with the toy lawn-mower in Barbados all those years ago. *Wow!* Imagine . . . imagine. Just keep pushing, never give up. Know that as long as you want something bad enough, even if you are not necessarily the best in the world, you just need to put the hard work in, keep good people around you and just keep pushing and you will get there. If I hadn't met Ashley and taken up his invitation to go to the studio, I would probably still be singing in the shower. Without the boys I would never have been able to get to where I am now and for that I am very blessed.

MYLES: Every day I wake up and think, *This is my life!* I genuinely count every second as a blessing. I am so grateful for all of it, every single moment. Yes, we have worked incredibly hard, and we will continue to do so every second of every day, but I feel blessed. I feel lucky to have met the boys and to be able to perform in a band with my brothers. I'm striving for us to succeed, to make this band as brilliant as it can be, to write songs we are proud of, to work hard and tour and play our music to as many people as possible.

We are trying to make music that is going to inspire people and make them want to hear more. We are going to do a tour with Little Mix in stadiums, we are working with some of the best producers and writers out there – it is such a privilege.

'If we work hard enough, always treat people with respect and spend every waking moment being the best we can be, then the world truly is our oyster. I just want the four of us to inspire people to follow their dreams and passions!'

MUS: My dream, my passion, was always to dance, and I feel like I've done that. However, what Rak-Su has done for me is give me the chance to be on the inside of songwriting, to help the guys create music that people love and that means something to them. I am really enjoying the vocal coaching we are having and being around so many talented engineers and producers in the studio. I am also working on my DJ skills and learning more about production, too. That is a very exciting prospect for the future, to be a part of that process. I want Rak-Su to be as big and as successful as possible. If we work hard enough, always treat people with respect and spend every waking moment being the best we can be, then the world truly is our oyster. I just want the four of us to inspire people to follow their dreams and passions!

MYLES: We have so much to do. We are out of *The X Factor* now, that is all over. There is the real world out there, and we have to earn our place in that. We have to become Rak-Su 2.0 and make sure that everything is on point at all times. All these amazing opportunities cannot be taken for granted, and they won't be. What a journey it has been, and it's proof to us that with some talent, a lot of hard work and a bit of self-belief, you can achieve anything.

THANKS

We never thought we would be writing the acknowledgements for our auto-biography! There are so many people we would like to thank for making this possible. Special thanks to our publishing team at Michael Joseph. Particularly to Dan Bunyard, Yasmin Morrissey, Sarah Fraser, Alice Chandler, David Ettridge, Liz Smith, Claire Bush, Ellie Hughes, Annabel Wilson, Louise Jones, Olivia Thomas, Nick Lowndes and Alice Mottram. To our team at Modest! Management: Richard Griffiths, Harry Magee, Samantha Cox and Andy Dutnall. To Simon Cowell, Louis Walsh, Nicole Scherzinger, Sharon Osbourne, Dermot O'Leary and everyone over at Syco and X Factor (too many to name but all just as important as each other). To Martin Roach, Eddie Serrano, Annabel Williams, Brahim Fouradi, Afterhrs, Ricky Valentine, Jordan Gutteridge, Hus Hodja, Riccardo VDC, Ashley Harewood, Alex 'Six' Safaris, Deanna Chase, Radhika Wilson & Superlative Sessions, Vivian Nwonka, Pauline Briscoe, Gemma Wheatcroft, Nadu Placca, Max Howe, Luke Lentes, Laurie Cunningham, Saoud Khalaf, Jamie Farrelly, James Hype, Ben Calnan, Callum Mills, Andy Bonura, Ollie Mattis, Jay Stephenson, Bobo Kijac, Jules 'Moko', Leigh Putman, Abe Jarman, Zak 'HipHop Dad', Dan Murray, John Eager, Nathan Barrow, Johno Jay, Mitchell Burton, Beth Renphrey, Clarence Mandisodza, Holly Jones, Lara McCabe, Scott Mckay and the UMA crew. And last but certainly not least, to you, the fans, for making this all possible.

PICTURE CREDITS

The publisher is grateful for permission to reproduce the images on the following pages:

Rak-Su's own on pages 18, 23, 26, 47, 59, 61, 78, 88–9, 103, 109, 114, 154, 158, 165, 190, 200, 227, 230, 231, 245, 248 & 275; © Callum Mills on pages 2–3, 4–5, 6–7, 13, 14–15, 20–21, 24, 25, 30, 32, 33, 34–5, 37, 38–9, 43, 44, 50, 51, 54–5, 56, 57, 58, 62–3, 64, 65, 67, 68–9, 77, 82–3, 84, 85, 86–7, 92, 95, 96, 97, 98, 99, 105, 106–7, 110–11, 122, 124–5, 126, 127, 129, 134, 138–9, 142–3, 145, 149, 157, 167, 171, 174, 183, 184–5, 186, 188, 196–7, 280–81 & 287; © Dan Kennedy on pages 28, 29, 70, 113, 130, 195, 208, 210–11, 240, 243, 247, 249, 253, 264–5, 276, 277, 278–9 & 284–5; © FremantleMedia/Simco Ltd on pages 192, 193, 206–7, 209, 215, 216–7, 220, 228, 233, 236–7, 238–9, 254, 258, 260, 269, 270, 271, 272 & 273; © Andy Bonura on pages 16, 40, 41, 48–9, 52, 53, 60, 74, 80, 116–17, 136–7, 180–81, 225 & 282; © Keaton Richardson on pages 19, 27, 90, 91 & 115; © Luke Lentes on pages 72–3, 133, 152–53 & 162–63; © Tom Cockram on pages 101 & 121. Every effort has been made to ensure images are correctly attributed; however, if any omission or error has been made please notify the publisher for correction in future editions.

webrokethesofa

MICHAEL JOSEPH

UK | USA | Canada | Ireland | Australia
India | New Zealand | South Africa

Michael Joseph is part of the Penguin Random House group of companies
whose addresses can be found at global.penguinrandomhouse.com

First published 2018
001

Text copyright © Rak-Su, 2018

For picture credits see page 286.

The moral right of the authors has been asserted

Set in F37 Ginger, Dream Team Thicker, Litera, Madera
Colour reproduction by Altaimage Ltd
Printed in Italy by Printer Trento

A CIP catalogue record for this book is available from the British Library

ISBN: 978–0–241–36458–1

www.greenpenguin.co.uk

MIX
Paper from
responsible sources
FSC® C018179

Penguin Random House is committed to a
sustainable future for our business, our readers
and our planet. This book is made from Forest
Stewardship Council® certified paper.